on $5,000,
$10,000, or
$25,000 a Day

Hollywood

on $5,000, $10,000, or $25,000 a Day

THE SURVIVAL GUIDE FOR LOW-BUDGET FILMMAKERS

By Philip Gaines and David J. Rhodes

SILMAN-JAMES PRESS
LOS ANGELES

First edition

10 9 8 7 6 5 4 3 2 1

Library of Congress Cataloging-in-Publication Data

Gaines, Philip.
Hollywood on $5,000, $10,000, or $25,000 a day : a survival
guide for low-budget filmmakers / Philip Gaines
and David J. Rhodes
p.   cm.
Includes bibliographical references.
1. Motion Pictures—Production and direction. 2. Low budget
motion pictures. I. Rhodes, David J. II. Title.
PN1995.9.P7G34 1994   791.43'0232—dc20   94-10051

ISBN: 1-879505-16-9

Cover Design by Heidi Frieder

Printed and bound in the United States of America

Silman-James Press
distributed by Samuel French Trade
7623 Sunset Blvd., Hollywood, CA 90046

CONTENTS

ACKNOWLEDGMENTS

Many fellow filmmakers helped with this endeavor and most of them would like to remain anonymous. We can hardly blame them. We'd have remained anonymous ourselves but for the egotistical need to see our names on the spine of a book sitting on the shelf in our local store.

Some brave souls do deserve mention for providing us with certain pieces of insider information. From the vendor collection we thank Scott Smith at Panavision, Mike De Lorenzo at Filmtrucks, and a host of folks at Fotokem. Made with the union label, thanks to Pat and Debbie (no last names, please) at SAG and Maureen Fleming at the AMPTP. From cast and crew and those old-devil distributors, we should single out in no particular order Dena Roth, Mark Yellen, Robert Hernandez, Rainer Stonus, Artie "Get a Grip on It" Smith, Marcus DeLeon, Sharon "Mae" West, the Polish Vamp's bro, Eddie Deezen, and Cassian Elwes; also Dan Hassid at Cineville; Marc Fischer, late of Cannon; Ellen Steloff, late of Vestron; Liz McDermott, still at Overseas (as of this writing anyway), and Siobhan McDevitt of Concord/New Horizons.

Of course, no acknowledgments would be complete without a nod to Mr. Blue Pencil, Jim Fox, and Gwen Feldman at Silman-James, who are putting our names on that spine.

PREFACE

Do I contradict myself?
Very well then I contradict myself
(I am large, I contain multitudes.)
　　　　　　　Walt Whitman, *Leaves of Grass*

This book is about how to make movies cheaply. This is a subject that contains a lot of inherent contradictions, because moviemaking and its related technology is inherently costlier than any other of the plastic arts. Tangentially, this book is about how to make movies that sell, hopefully not for cheap. It's not about how to get the money to make movies, cheap or otherwise. If you're looking for that type of information, get one of the books about that. We'd have put them into the Bibliography, but here's the thing: We make movies, we know how to raise money for them, and there's enough competition for what dollars there are already. Do your own legwork on that one.

　　Okay, let's assume you've got the wherewithal to make the movie and would like some tips on how to hold down costs. A lot of the information in this book, especially about how to get things for little or no money, is most effective if the movie you're making has some small shred of redeeming social value. In other words, the artier the better. If you're planning some topless, teenage beach romp or a good, old-fashioned, axe-in-the-face, chop-'em-up, maybe you should save what little money you have for blood or body make-up and not blow ten bucks on this book.

Now, if you're still reading and have gotten to paragraph three, we hope it's because you bought this book, took it home, put your feet up, got a cold one of choice, and are ready to absorb some serious, inside information. Because this book is not about how to make a movie—God knows there are dozens of books about that, chock full of charts and glossaries and a lot of other useless junk. We've got a whole section talking about them so that you won't waste your time or dollars on a really useless one. Like we said in the very first sentence: This book is about how to make movies cheaply.

All right, enough banter. We're not writing because we love the soft clicking sound of the computer keyboard or to build up the page count. The information that we propose to share with you is frank and to the point. The first movie we made was back in the mid-'80s, when cash flowed freely out of Europe and Japan and video deals for real schlock easily broke seven figures. It (the movie) cost about $26,000, up-front cash, and a ton in deferments, which we assume nobody is still expecting to get. It had a couple of tired old TV-name actors of the Will (Sugarfoot) Hutchins school, who will keep showing up on sets for a few thou and a free lunch until they've lost all their hair and teeth, and then they'll probably switch to playing drooling psychos. This was not an easy-lopin', cattle-ropin' experience; but more on that later.

Those days are gone. The "seven figures for real schlock" part, not the deferred work or the drooling psychos part. Actually, we should qualify that, because it is possible to get big bucks for pricey schlock. It's the cheap schlock that won't get anything but low-end video sales in today's global market. But you can still make a feature motion picture, as advertised on the cover, for 5,000, 10,000 or 25,000 dollars a day. Multiply that by your shooting days and it translates to a total price tag ranging from a low of fifty Gs to a high of six-and-a-quarter (i.e., $625,000). If that's your ballpark, this is the book for you. Even if you have more to spend, there are plenty of tips that are certainly worth your while. We'd almost be willing to guarantee that if you made your movie after reading this book and you didn't save hundreds or thousands of dollars as a result, we'd give you your money back. But, hey, we're not stupid. On the other hand, if you do save all that money and are so overwhelmed with gratitude that you'd like to offer us a little bonus check as a token of appreciation, don't be shy! Send it c/o the publishers with a laudatory letter, so that, when you get famous, we can quote you on the back of future editions.

We are now at the end of the Preface. If you are still reading while standing in the movie section of a discount bookstore in some mall, either put this book down before it gets too dog-eared to sell or do the smart thing: Take it up to the front register, buy it, and read it in the privacy of your own abode.

CHAPTER ONE

"It is certainly rather a curious production," said
Holmes. "At first sight it would appear to be some
childish prank . . . Why should you attribute any
importance to so grotesque an object?"
Arthur Conan Doyle, *The Dancing Men*

FADE IN. The books begins. That's right, "Fade In." Not
"Smash Cut To" or some other bogus attempt at a dy-
namic opening. The beginning is not about artifice or
manipulation, it's about one simple question: Why do you
want to make this movie? If, by some incredible oversight,
you have not yet asked yourself that question, now is the
time. We can't hear your answer, and in any case, you
certainly don't need our permission (or anyone else's) to
proceed, so you might as well as be honest. We can only
hope that somewhere in your reply is the statement or,
at least the implication, that you want to make or already
do make movies because movies are your life. This is no
joke. We've already assumed that you're not reading this
book because you did not score high enough on the civil-
service exam to be a mail carrier and producing seemed
like a good second choice. And please, to any postal-
service persons who read or hear of this statement, don't
start redirecting our mail to Anchorage. We are not dis-
paraging anyone, not lawyers, not insurance agents, not
even politicians. Our only point is that, whether you think
of filmmaking as a job, a profession, a lifestyle, or a mis-
sion from God, it requires an amount of dedication that
we would have to describe as above average. Like

Sherlock said, movies, particularly low-budget ones, are curious productions. If they do sometimes resemble childish pranks or grotesque objects, that is the shortcoming of the filmmakers, which, if movies are your life, must be what you are or what you want to be.

You may have noticed by now that the Authors (hereinafter "we") are directly addressing the Filmmakers (hereinafter "you"). Yes, *we*, as writers and filmmakers, do have egos that are also above average. But *we* are talking to *you* in a direct style because (1) we want to keep the confusion out of our discourse, and (2) we want you to think about *what* we have to say, not *how* we say it.

So, why do you want to make this movie? We all know that short Hollywood answer: "Because I believe in this project." Guess what? That's not only the Hollywood answer, it is, as far as any six words can be, also the right answer. But why do you believe in this project? Why do you "love" this script? Because it will make a good movie? That would be great, and in an ideal world, it might also be true. The more fundamental issue is, Will it make a movie and will it be a movie that anyone else will want to see? Of equal importance: Can you make this movie with the amount of money that you have available?

We'll get deeper into that shortly, but, as we said, the other assumption of this book is that you've got the money. It probably took a lot of cajoling and a lot more luck and will make for a lot of great stories later when you're accepting some life achievement award. But now, before you start actually making the movie, you've got to remember how you found the hook. And if somebody just happened to dump the money in your lap, you've still got to find the hook now and dust off your SAG card. When we say that you've got to find the hook, it means simply that you must find the aspect(s) of your production that most appeals to each individual and present it with whatever embellishments are necessary and appropriate to snare that person and keep him or her on the end of your line.

Dust off your SAG card? What this means is that, even though you may not be a member of the Screen Actors Guild (if not, you might want to consider giving yourself a small part so that you can join, because, after all, the dues are low and you can buy SAG jackets as nifty holiday gifts for the folks and friends; but we digress), this is show business, you are the filmmaker, and you've got to play the part. In order to convince your collaborators in the production process to join your endeavor and in order to keep them focused and motivated, you will have to constantly reinforce whatever concepts made them decide to sign up in the first place.

Don't misunderstand us. We are not talking about some phony epithets borrowed from the catechism of fledgling agents. We are not telling you to unfasten another button on your shirt, start a calling people "babe," or buy a silver-plated cellular phone that passes for a cigarette case. If there is nothing in your project that appeals to people, no amount of feathers or fish eggs will make them strike at your lure.

Since neither of us is a fisherman, it's probably time to retire this analogy. But the point remains: Much if not most of producing is salesmanship, pure and simple. But when you're worn out, depressed, and down to the last few dollars in your production account, the image you need in your mind is not Willy Loman trudging off with his sample cases in defeat but David O. Selznick hoisting an Oscar over his head in triumph.

Low-budget moviemaking really is all about "imaging" techniques. Winning athletes imagine themselves hitting the tape first or sending one over the fence. Filmmaking home runs take a little longer—almost as long as the slo-mo paean that concludes *The Natural* (but hopefully without as much sparking and breaking of glass).

Organizing Principles

> Making motion pictures is really a matter of
> organization. First, you must organize your
> mind, then you must organize the people
> around you so that everyone is telling
> the same story.
>
> Henry King

Who was Henry King? If you don't know and haven't
found out by the time you get to Chapter Three, we'll tell
you there. There was a book published a few years ago
called *Feature Filmmaking At Used Car Prices*. We will
talk more about it, and a lot of other books, in the Appendix; but we bring it up here to evoke one end of the
vast range of feature-film costs. We're not sure what kind
of used car you can get for $6,000, but you can make a
feature. When one of us was in high school, a couple of
classmates got together and shot an 8mm feature about
anxiety and adolescence. A couple of parents chipped in
$250, and the end result was nearly eighty minutes long
(talk about teenage *angst*), with dialogue and music
dubbed onto a magstripe on the edge of the film. $250—
is that an all-time low? Who knows. What's the most ever
spent? The Russian-made *War and Peace* reportedly cost
over $150 million (and over a hundred lives filming the
battle scenes) back in the early '60s. It's taken Hollywood
a while to flirt with the $100 million mark, and a dollar
isn't worth quite as much these days. But, in fairness, *War
and Peace* was nearly sixteen hours long, and *Terminator 2* is only a couple.

What if we remade *War and Peace*? It's public domain, so there's no three million to pay for rights like a
current best-seller. But we pay William Goldman $3.5
million to adapt—that's a lot but we hear it's really a long
book—then bring in Joe Eszterhas to steam it up for an-

other 2. Got to have an action director. John Badham? No, old hat. We'll get John McTiernan, that's $6 million. Cast should be the best Hollywood has to offer: Alec Baldwin, Sharon Stone, Tom Cruise, Julia Roberts (maybe we can get a package deal with a song from Lyle Lovett), some character part for Pacino or Dustin Hoffman, and, of course, Gene Hackman as the old general who beats the pants off Napoleon. Or does Napoleon beat the pants off him? Napoleon—maybe we could get Brando instead of Hackman. Whatever, maybe we can coax Harrison Ford down from Montana—no, wait, what were we thinking? It's an action picture with some introspection. It's got to be big, so we need Arnold as Pierre. It's a long shooting schedule, but it's also art, so we can get him for $20 million plus gross points. Hope he doesn't burst the seams on those tight-fitting tail coats. So we've spent $60 or $70 million before even thinking about building a Russian ballroom or burning Moscow. Clearly, there is no maximum that can be spent on a single movie.

We've done the flip-side. We've written the script in a few days, called in favors from crew members with their own equipment, shot on weekends, made lists of what props and cars we had or knew about so we could use those. We've kept an eye out for cops because we didn't have permits and kept our fingers crossed, hoping that the cheapest lab in Hollywood wouldn't ruin footage shot on short ends that somebody had in the garage for a year or two because we could never afford to buy insurance to cover us against scratches and other screw-ups. You can read a bunch of heartfelt anecdotes in *Feature Film-making at Used Car Prices*. What we want to sketch in briefly are the Organizing Principles from which these tales of guerrilla filmmaking derive.

The first may seem obvious, but you'd be surprised how many people forget: Count your money. That's not how much you would like to have or how much you think you'll get. That's how much is in the bank or guaranteed to come in. You have to know this figure before you can go on to Step Two.

Step Two. Set your goal. There are only two choices: (1) Spend all you have getting the picture in the can, i.e., shoot it now and somehow get the money to finish it later. Or (2) budget the money so that you can get all the way to a finished picture. You think there are other choices? You've heard that some people spend all their money shooting and finishing a complete scene or two from their movie, then use that to go out and raise the rest. Sure, that happens. And it works as often as there are babies born on February 29th. This is not a good concept. In fact, Option 1 is not really a good concept. Anything less than a finished film leaves you at the mercy of those investors who want to be "last in, first out" or, worse yet, distributors. When investors and distributors smell blood in the water, it's not pretty.

Step Three is dividing up how the cash and other resources will be spent, also known as "budgeting." (Is this the information you've been waiting for? Relax. We're a couple of chapters away from budgeting line-by-line; this is a full-length book, not a short subject). Since all we're discussing right here are the organizing principles, the key phrase is "cash and other resources." Mainstream budgets, even those at the high end of the 5, 10, and 25 spectrum, which often have banks and completion-bond reps looking over their shoulders, must deal in cash only. There, when the script calls for any item, be it person, place, or thing, the budgeting process translates that item into dollars. On what we like to call the micro-budget, it is advisable, even necessary, to make a list of what you already have. This may be few rolls of gel or gaffer's tape lying around in your garage or an actor friend who promised to throw in a day or two's work if you ever got around to making that feature you've been talking about. Making movies, like any manufacturing process, consists of expending capital. And capital, we all know, consists not just of money but also of durable goods (expendables and machinery) and labor.

In the micro-budget, a zero-dollar entry can either mean that you don't need that person, place, or thing or that you know it can be had for zero dollars. Film production is labor intensive, and labor is the easiest thing to have for zero dollars. It's hard to walk down a street in Hollywood without tripping over an out-of-work grip. And once that grip agrees to work for "gas money" (after all, what else is he or she doing besides lying around getting tripped over?), maybe the deal can include the taco cart in the grip's garage. (If you think we mean this grip moonlights as a street vendor, you'd best check the Glossary.)

All other organizing principles are the standard ones of the industry, and all flow from this assessment process and the script itself. We are not saying that you should start by sitting down, making a list of what you have, and writing a script to fit. Certainly that's worked for some people, e.g., the author of *Feature Filmmaking at Used Car Prices*; but the process should be a little more flexible than that.

Imagination, it's funny . . .

And if imagination could make a cloudy day sunny, it would rate a lot higher with directors of photography.

Much as we hate to admit it (because, if you couldn't already tell, we're not really writers), the imagination that starts it all belongs to the screenwriter or the novelist or yellow journalist or whoever wrote the first words that end up as a movie. But the "vision," as Hollywood has told us over and over, belongs to the filmmakers, the producers, and directors who take these scribblings and breathe movie life into them.

We must also admit, and we do so ungrudgingly, that

writers cannot be expected to create scenes and flesh out characters while constantly worrying about how much it will cost to shoot their material. We're not talking about that apocryphal one-eighth of a script page that reads "World War II begins." We're talking about the fact that if the scene is a press conference and Reporters Number 1 through 6 each ask a question, that is four actor-day checks more than if Reporters 1 and 2 asked three questions each. Here's the math:

6 x $485 SAG scale + 10% agent allowance = $ 3,201
2 reporters = $1,067

This is also assuming that the actors work eight hours or less. A safe assumption you say? Sure, if everything goes as planned, if the scene isn't scheduled after one that takes a lot longer than anyone imagined, and those guys weren't called in a little early just in case the first scene went faster than anyone imagined; and they end up sitting around on the clock for six hours before even rehearsing the scene, and then the sun goes down and they all have to come back the next day! We're not exaggerating all that much, but you get the point. Now, you say that's all part of the process, that's what contingencies and overtime allowances are for. Well, on 5, 10, or even 25 thou a day, those won't go very far.

And what about the "hidden" costs? How about the 12.65% union fringe and 18% or 19% government fringe, including workmen's comp? And the cost of processing six payments instead of two? How about four more rooms in a honeywagon, four more meals, four more mileage and wardrobe allowances? This stuff adds up. What's the point of the scene anyway? How many people ask questions? How many non-actor friends of the producer (or producers themselves) get a moment on screen, and how many Taft-Hartley fines does SAG later levy for these shenanigans at $400 a pop? Or is this scene about the lead actor's responses to those questions? Does it matter how many different reporters make these penetrating queries?

How about if just two people ask them and you cast some friends who are already paid-up SAG members and they agree to work for "fringes only"? (More on that later.)

And while we're at it, does this scene have to be on the steps of City Hall at high noon? Do we have to rent an expensive location, hire cops to hold traffic, take a whole company downtown, and then pray that we don't get rained on? Why can't the mayor, the councilman, the police chief, the head dog catcher, whoever he or she is, hold this press conference at the office or the station or the animal shelter, somewhere with a lot less extras and inconvenience? No, not the real animal shelter with the barking dogs and the walls that echo with every crepe-soled step and the dark recesses that are so hard to light. Something that looks like an animal shelter, with a sign on it that says so, something we cut to after an establishing shot of a real animal shelter that you sent two or three guys and not the whole company out to shoot sometime and you didn't even bother to get a permit to do it. Imagination. It's funny. It's how movies are made. It's also how money is saved.

Picking the Script

> It has all the freshness and vigor, but also a full measure of the faults, of a hasty production.
> Miguel de Cervantes, *Don Quixote*

The difference between what the writer imagines, what the director imagines, and what the producer imagines may be quite substantial, so let's set the rules. Unless he or she is also the producer or director (and, yes, that is the case in a lot of low-budget movies), once the script is done, what the writer imagined does not matter at all. What matters is how the director and producer imagine the movie. In a high-budget Hollywood world, if it says "High in the Alps," they used to go to the back lot or a sound stage and now they go to the Alps. In a medium-budget world, it's rewritten for the Rockies. In a low-budget world, a local location in the Angeles Forest or Big Bear stands in. And, of course, in the micro-budget, you find someone who has a house with a lot of big rocks in the back yard.

It is up to the filmmakers to make decisions of this sort for every item in the script. So the best way for those on a budget to prevent problems is never to pick a script that's got "High in the Alps" written anywhere in it.

The budget range we're addressing in this book means that feature filmmakers will be able to afford between ten and thirty days of shooting. Let's use twenty as a mean. Even if the locations are local—and let's make clear that another assumption is that interiors will also be shot as practicals, i.e., inside an actual location—thirty to forty of them must mean that a good part of every day will be used moving from one place to another, time in which the talents of all the crew except the drivers are being wasted.

Because quality and quantity are both critical factors, every script element has to be analyzed from both perspectives. As with locations, the type and number of roles is a key cost factor. On a micro-budget, "official" use of members of the Screen Actors Guild may not be possible. Official means signing the SAG Basic Agreement, posting a bond, and adhering to its terms, which govern everything from the number of casting callbacks to the distance one can ask an actor to drive to a location. If the actors, SAG or non-SAG, are being paid, the more of them there are, the more it costs. Not just the more there are in the whole script, but in individual scenes as well. Thirty actors for a couple of days each (sixty man-days) is a lot cheaper than five actors for the run of the show (ignoring for the sake of simplicity that SAG weekly scale is cheaper than five times daily scale, that's roughly five times twenty days or 100 man-days). If a scene has two actors doing meaningful dialogue and two others sitting around nodding, why? And if you have to have four people in a scene, remember, that doesn't just mean four paydays instead of two. It may also mean the time to set up, light, and photograph close-ups of four faces instead of two.

What does all this mean? Are these guidelines that should be given to the screenwriters? Not really. The reality of most micro-budget productions is that, while many are made from formula scripts concocted just for the purpose of filling a ninety-minute video, we know that most non-exploitation scripts are written by earnest dramaturges who would find such issues as how many car crashes or how many actors too restrictive of their art. In all seriousness, as we implied above, writers should write, producers should produce, and so on ad nauseam. This brings us back to the initial concept. First, pick a script that is not impossibly difficult to accomplish with the money you have. Second, work with the writer, director, or anyone else who knows how to ply a blue pencil to remove extraneous scenes and characters.

Rules to Live By

> The production of spectacular effects depends more on the art of the stage machinist than on that of the poet.
> Aristotle, *Poetics*

For those who must have a list of precepts, here they are. Please remember, we are continuing to assume that you would prefer to make a good movie and not just fill a garish video box for quick profit.

1) Dramas are preferable to comedies. Comedies require more ensemble moments, timing, on-set rehearsal, and/or silly props. Unless you are making a parody in which cheap sets and inappropriate costumes are part of the humor, comedies require more time and money. We'll discuss such exceptions to the rule as *A Polish Vampire in Burbank* in a later chapter, but overall, the tone and setting of the "serious" film, from horrific to neo-realistic, place fewer demands on time and resources.

2) Contemporary settings are preferable to period settings. Big surprise here. Certain period films, such as the Western, may benefit from a spare look, as with the Monte Hellman pictures from the '60s, *The Shooting* and *Ride the Whirlwind.* These pictures used nearby locations and a small cast as well as following Precept #3. Typically, however, the contemporary setting is right outside the door of the office waiting to be photographed. The period setting is waiting to be designed, dressed, costumed, and then struck—harder to do with no money. When settings are naturalistic, all that may be required from a production-design standpoint is finding a workable location.

3) Five Day Players (that's five people for one day each) are preferable to adding a single actor on a Picture Deal. As we said before, unless the entire shooting schedule is less than one week, one or two leads and a host of supporting players who come on for one or two days is optimal.

4) One location is preferable to Two. (Or Three or Twelve or . . . you get the point.) This doesn't mean the fewest sets. One location, such as a mansion (and, yes, budget mansions can be found), can yield a dozen sets ranging from a kitchen to a ballroom to a boudoir. For practical purposes, "one location" means any place where the crew does not have to put the equipment back onto the trucks in order to get to the next set, so that a gas station immediately adjacent to restaurant that is two

doors down from a flower shop may constitute three sets in one location.

5) Exteriors are preferable to Interiors (the capital "I" is for stylistic balance; no allusions to Woody Allen are intended). Alternate precept: Available light is preferable to lighting any scene. Sunlight is free. Shiny boards (for the uninitiated, reflectors are used to bounce light onto actors' faces, particularly in Westerns) are little more than aluminum foil stretched over big pieces of cardboard. Indoors, actors posed pensively by unshuttered windows may not only look more artful, it's faster and cheaper than setting up a light. Even ordinary lights—this does not mean 100-watt bulbs but traditional, DC-powered Tungsten movie lights as opposed to daylight-balanced, AC-powered HMI lights—require a substantial amount of amperage, three or four times more than the 60 to 150 amps in a normal home or office. This means generators, fuel to run them, engine noise to be baffled, and probably $37.50 per hour (time and half after eight) plus fringes for a Fire Safety Officer to ensure that no passersby are menaced and that no buildings are burned down because such devices are in use. And while a small HMI light may occasionally be plugged into an ordinary household outlet, tapping into the box of any building without the necessary permits and personnel invites disaster. Not only is sunlight free, but the great outdoors lack ceilings, corners, doorways, stairwells, and those other constraints on the movement of actors and camera and the placement of microphones. Sure, it may rain or cloud over or be noisier, but it makes it a whole lot easier to get light through a cheap zoom lens with a high f-stop onto a small piece of film. Most scripts will contain Exteriors and Interiors, so the writers get to follow in tradition and put EXT and INT at the beginning of each new scene; and, except for Westerns, most movies will need a mix of the two. But the ratio of one to the other and the nature of the Interiors are key factors in scheduling

(lighting and decorating time) and budgeting (time is money).

6) A location that works for Camera is preferable to a location that works for Sound. If you understand this sentence, give yourself a bonus point because you're thinking ahead, and that's what low-budget filmmakers do. The bottom line is that you can replace lines of dialogue in a soundproof booth at some later date. You can't replace the image. Trying to repair it by, for instance, optically removing some inappropriate item from the edge of the frame is a costly process. At best, it also slightly deteriorates the image. The lines substituted by an actor at a looping session may sound better from not only a noise standpoint but for performance as well. This may not be the ideal spot for an extended aside about actors, but we feel like saying it now, so here goes: Nothing, not the cheapest sets, the fuzziest image, or the most unintelligible sound makes a picture seem lower budget than bad acting. Bad acting doesn't even work in comedies because it is not inherently funny, and the "joke" gets old pretty fast. Sure, *Plan Nine From Outer Space* or Edgar G. Ulmer's rarer and even funnier *Girls in Chains* may be the most uproarious unintentional "comedies" ever made. So what. Such cosmic misalignments of filmic elements from ridiculous scripting to skewed editing rarely occur.

Back to the point, which was already a tangent: Bad acting looks and sounds cheap. But just like Kuleshov discovered in that legendary moment back at the dawn of filmmaking time when he intercut the same close-up of an actor with different point-of-view shots and alternately drew both tears and laughter from the audience (yes, we are being hyperbolic, because what Kuleshov really did was make it seem that the actor, some great thespian, the Russian equivalent of John Barrymore, was evoking pity when he "looked" at a dying man, anger when he saw a dog being maltreated, joy at a child playing, and hunger over a bowl of Cheetos, none of which examples is exactly as we've described because we just made them up since we don't have the time or inclination to pour through reference books for the exact images but we remember the gist of the experiment and these are good analogs and here comes the close parenthesis before this turns into the longest non-fiction sentence ever written), filmmakers of the sound era realize that they can put just about any replacement words into any actor's mouth.

We're not talking about Woody Allen's *What's Up Tiger Lily* but Glenn Close "voicing" the pre-*sex, lies, and videotape* performance of Andie MacDowell in *Greystoke*. Even the garage filmmaker can accomplish the same sleight-of-hand as David ("Big budget, take forever to get the shot") Lean did when he replaced all of Christopher Jones' vocal performance in *Ryan's Daughter*. So while Lean may have encouraged Sarah Miles to goose Jones at the critical juncture of the love scene to get the expression he wanted, the sound could wait till later.

This actually takes us back to the point of Precept #6, but we've got another helpful hint. Those wild and crazy actors and technicians who worked at Cinecitta in the '50s and '60s will—more than the wildly out-of-synch lips in the average Japanese-to-English movie that Allen parodied or the absurdly off sound effects in any Mexican horror flick transformed by K. Gordon Murray in Coral Gables, Florida—forever epitomize the cheap dub. But what they proved is that, lacking the almost perfect dialogue replacement that made *Das Boot* into *The Boat*, the viewer's mind will accommodate. Dialogue that is continually out of the sync because the sound loop on the projector is too small is unsettling and unacceptable. Dialogue that slips in and out of sync because of the exigencies of looping can get by. Dead sync between image and sound is just a convention, anyway. Even television news shows regularly pull up the sound of explosions on the horizon so that they seem to be "in sync," but anyone who has ever watched a fireworks display or seen lightning and then heard thunder knows that this is not reality, that light and sound reach the distant observer at separate intervals. What "sells" a percussive sound effect from a car door slamming to a gunshot is dead sync, as tight and easy to do by the greenest assistant editor as matching the clapper and the sound blob in dailies. What sells atmospheric effects from the wind howling to the squishing sound of car tires on wet streets is the audience expectation. They make the sight and sound work together and sync references are secondary. Because dialogue is much less percussive than gunshots or door slams, the audience will give it a great deal of leeway, and voice replacement can be a cheap fix when you discover on the set that you've cast a stiff.

7) Silent scenes are preferable to talking ones. No, we're not being silly. Most movies, regardless of budget, contain a significant amount of time when people and/ or objects are visible on screen but no dialogue is heard. Obviously, we're not suggesting that every one should aspire to variants of *The Thief*, a quirky spy film from 1952 with Ray Milland as a foreign agent that contains no dialogue whatsoever, or *Daughter of Horror*, a psychological horror flick with no conversation but plenty of atmosphere. Those with some smattering of experience watching silent films must know that meaning can indeed be conveyed without words. We're not going to start off on some obscure line of argument that suggests that the coming of sound killed off true cinema; but think about it. Think about all those silent sequences from Hitchcock, like James Stewart following Kim Novak around San Francisco or, for true aficionados, Tippi Hedren stealing the money from Sean Connery's company. This is the kind of filmmaking that wins awards (not at the time in Hitchcock's case, of course, so let's say "accolades written in French"), that gets you enshrined in critical pan-

theons, that wows agents and producers whom you would like to package your next, mainstream feature, and that saves money, too. What could be better?

8) Talking about shipwrecks is preferable to shooting shipwrecks. Yes, we are exaggerating slightly, but the idea is sound. Obviously, a script in which characters sit around and talk about one exciting event after another is either a comedy (see Precept #1) or is going to have its brass fasteners removed before it gets tossed into the bin of recycled copy paper. If you can build an entire movie talking about a bank robbery that is never seen, as in *Reservoir Dogs*, that's great. What we mean is, you won't be shooting any shipwrecks on a micro-budget, not even in a studio tank with 1/5-scale miniatures that look pretty hokey, anyway. Not even in your bathtub with a plastic kit model of the Titanic, unless it's a comedy (see Precept #1 again). So if you cannot avoid shipwrecks altogether (far and away the best alternative), all you can afford is for a couple of characters to talk about how traumatic it was for little Cindy to have Mom and the family dog lost at sea.

9) Two people talking in a scene is preferable to three (or four or five, etc.) people talking or to two people talking with three (or four or five, etc.) people who talk elsewhere in the movie sitting around and listening to them. We kind of said this already in the press conference example, but this is the official precept list and the point bears repeating. What all these freeform precepts are meant to do is open your mind to the alternate possibilities in every scene of every script that you may be considering for production, and Precept #9 is taken from that stereotypical tag line in trailers past that promised "a cast of thousands." As we already know, actors cost money, not just in salaries, but from dressing rooms for them to sit in and wardrobe for them to wear down to make-up for their faces, lunches for them to eat, and extra script copies for them to read. Save resources and don't throw

an actor into a scene unless there is a purpose for his or her being there.

10) The unexpected is preferable to the expected. The details on this precept are tied in to "theory," to the way in which filmmakers and film viewers interact, a concept over which so many people with doctorates in film (still a hard concept for those of us who think "film doctors," like "script doctors," are guys who come in after the first guy and perform the life saving surgery) have spilled so much ink. Let's talk about this "theory" as it relates to low and micro-budget movies.

Most viewers, whether seated in a theater or on a living-room sofa, know which end is up. They know what kind of picture they are watching from the trailers, the ad art (one sheet or video box), the stars, the director, all the hype that anticipates and surrounds any release, large or small. They can also tell from the style and substance of the above what the budget of the movie is, i.e., Arnold and Sly equal X dollars, Wings Hauser equals X cents.

Let's consider for a moment the biggest "flop" of Summer 1993, *The Last Action Hero*. What's the problem with this picture? Can you hear those folks at Columbia (not to mention Executive Producer Arnold) saying to the filmgoers, "Didn't we spend enough? $80 million couldn't hack it? Didn't we blow up enough stuff? Didn't Arnold and the kid go on enough talk shows?" Don't these guys get it? You can't spend eighty million dollars on a comedy. Hey, we think it's great. You've got expensive stunts and optical effects combined so that the viewer can watch a van cartwheel and explode, in the background! This takes guts. A gag that expensive, and you don't even see it up close.

Not a comedy, you say? Come on, does it or does it not contain two scenes with a chain-smoking, cartoon cat in a trench coat named Whiskers, who shoots a turncoat FBI agent named Practice (Intro line: "How do you get to Carnegie Hall?"), played by F. Murray Abraham so that the movie-wise kid can call him "the guy who killed Mozart"? Sure, having Arnold the character scoff when the kid tells him that it's all a movie and he's being played by "Arnold Braunschweiger" is not the world's greatest running gag. But it is a gag. And the audiences stayed away in droves because they couldn't fathom plucking down seven hard-earned bucks to see an $80 million comedy where a house blows up with Arnold and the kid inside, and we cut to the next scene, where they both resemble Wile E. Coyote after another Acme misfire. He isn't in the end credits, but Wile E. Coyote and Acme even make cameo appearances, and they still don't get it. You could put flashing arrows or laugh signs at the bottom of the screen, and they wouldn't accept it. The movie parodies big-budget action pictures so literally that it forgets that it's a big-budget action picture, which is just too schizophrenic for most viewers to sit through.

There's an old adage that Hollywood embraced long ago: Tell them what you're going to say, say it, then tell them what you said. Fine; but it doesn't work when you say something unacceptable, something that just doesn't add up. You must give an audience what it expects, and you can push the limits of that expectation only so far. But low-budget, those are different rules, right? Anything goes. Wrong. Can you put Linnea Quigley in a picture, have her keep all her clothes on throughout, and expect the rental tape to return unmangled? What would Joe Bob say? We can't use such language here. *sex, lies, and videotape*, including the cutesy, e.e. cummings-esque title, is about as far as one can go. It's a serious parody that works, not because it's low-budget but because it recognizes the limits imposed by what the viewer expects.

So how does this precept work? It works at the script stage, so that it helps to keep an open mind when reading unconventional material. It could work even more at the production stage. How? Consider some wild and improbable hypotheticals. A character, sane or insane, converses with an invisible companion. You frame the actor with empty space left and right and dub a voice later. Unexpected and cheap. A character has nightmare flashbacks. Do anything you want here. Cut in limbo scenes (no, not someone dancing under a bar to Caribbean music), make them underexposed or overexposed, fuzzy or sharp, put the character in front of backdrops that change at will, use whatever you have lying around. With video cameras being so omnipresent, take a page from *sex, lies, and videotape.* Have a character using a camcorder and cut in footage. But, please, whatever you do, don't use the Rodney King footage for the seven millionth time. The unexpected can be either funny (like imagination) or serious. If it's the former, don't spend eighty million bucks on it, okay?

11) Adults are preferable to children, who need to be accompanied by a parent or guardian, even if you're making a G-rated picture. Also by a welfare worker/ teacher, who needs a room in which to spend three hours a day instructing the children you hired. Needless to say, children are not permitted to pull a fourteen-hour shift or work well into the night, either. So, cute as they may be, micro-budgeteers should avoid them like they would last week's socks. Low-budget pictures can stand one or two minors for a couple of days, but anything more can mess up a schedule faster than Dennis the Menace uncombs his hair. Unless they have some value (e.g., some box-office appeal when they were little tykes à la Drew Barrymore or good TVQ), even emancipated minors can cause problems, especially if they cozy up with over-twenty-one co-workers, as actors in particular are prone to do. So, really, when that wide-eyed, dimply-cheeked, completely irresistible young thing wanders into your casting office, make sure you have enough money before you try to launch any careers.

12) Last and least, or rather less, which is more. Confused by our syntax, our meaning, and the lack of the

word preferable? How is less more? Since you have only so many dollars to spend, put them where they will show up the best. One well-known, quality actor is better than a host of lesser lights who were stars in the '50s and/or had their own sitcoms. We don't just mean that Clint Eastwood is better than Clint Walker! If you can get Clint, Arnold, or Jack, you don't need this book. We also don't mean that Edward James Olmos is better than Erik Estrada, but that is closer to our point. What we mean is that Forest Whitaker, although he doesn't really sell any tickets, is better than Richard Roundtree, that Rod Steiger is better than Tony Curtis, that Tim Roth is better than a phalanx of Wings Hausers or Anthony Gearys, and that anyone is better than Erik Estrada or Troy Donahue. If you don't get this, you haven't been spending enough time in video stores.

What this means is that you should spend your cast money as follows: Spend as much as it takes to get one "name" for the video box and whatever is left over for all the rest of the actors. The same applies to pretty much everything else. Okay, you have enough money to rent a dolly for the run of the show. But the occasional well-executed camera move is much better than a host of cheap, pointless ones. Not a lot of money for set decoration? A couple of pricey, lead props makes a greater impact than a ton of garage-sale, thrift-shop junk.

This is the big precept, and the most elusive one as well, because it involves a lot of subtle selection criteria. It is also what separates the filmmakers who make an impact with their micro-budget features from the perpetual wanna-bes, what separates Quentin Tarantino from Fred Olen Ray. (Sorry, Fred, nothing personal, babe. You're a class guy, even if you do run a museum of freakery on the side, but true is true.) If you don't know who these people are, take a break, and do a little research at your local Blockbuster.

CHAPTER TWO

Thus it is that Heaven, in the production of things, is sure to be bountiful to them, according to their qualities.

Confucius, *Doctrine of the Mean*

Budgeting and Scheduling

All right, you've got a script and you've got some money. Putting them together to make a movie involves lots of decisions and a plan of attack encapsulated in budgeting and scheduling. This book is not designed to teach you the physical act of budgeting and scheduling, but how to maximize the impact of your dollars over time and space.

We are going to embellish here on some of the issues raised in the first chapter, all of which have a direct impact on budget; but the line-item details are for Chapter Four.

In theory, low-budget scheduling is totally subsumed into cost considerations. Actor or location only available on certain days? Shoot them on those days. Not enough money for twenty-five days of equipment rental over five weeks. Shoot for twenty-four days over four weeks. God may have rested on the seventh day, but schedules for micro-budgets may have to forego that luxury and shoot on Sundays, too. Scheduling on the 5/10/25 framework has many decisions built in. Normally, one tries to cluster scenes at the same locations and scenes with the actor together; and it's a common type of conflict that requires finesse. If actors are all deferred but some locations cost money, there's nothing to finesse.

In the abstract and in the big-budget world, the balance of labor and material often tips toward labor. Where actors, directors, writers all work for abundant fees, relative value demands that the crew be in for large coin, too. In low- and micro-budgets, formulas such as relative value can be pretty useless. Labor that is 100% deferred is another matter. Actors and directors building showcase "reels" and crews made up of a lot of f.o.f.s. (fresh out of film school) looking for "experience projects"—these folks work long and hard for nothing. So their schedules don't count. Getting them together in Hollywood or anywhere is easy. Cutting the cost is harder if you're dealing with organized labor.

Guilds and Unions

Let's get one thing straight up front: Guilds and unions exist for good reason. Creative and technical people who work in the film industry have as much right as creative and technical people anywhere not to be exploited, either directly through up-front low pay or indirectly through reuse of their efforts in a host of extra markets without any residual compensation. We won't dwell on the old story about the man who cleans up after the elephants in the circus, but no amount of show-business glamour should convince anyone to work under terms or conditions that make them unhappy. But people do—and guilds and unions are there to give them some leverage.

Now the flip-side. Most of the creative people who want to work in films need to showcase their talent. Many writers, producers, directors, and actors will gladly toil for no money at all if it means getting their work up on screen. There is nothing wrong with this attitude, and there is nothing wrong with taking advantage of it. The problem is that, while most of the guilds and unions have formal or informal "low-budget" side letters, none of them has "micro-budget" side letters.

One of the most ridiculous examples is the Directors Guild of America formula. The DGA, anachronistically enough, still has a rate in its Basic Agreement for feature films "under $500,000." It calls for a "guaranteed" amount of prep, shooting, and cutting periods that total eleven weeks. The rate is $5,722 per week. Excuse us, but adding only the DGA fringes of 12.5%, that's over $70,000! That's more than 14% of the total budget! The cost of such staple items as cameras and the film and cast and food to put in them means that on any picture made for under half a million dollars, people must work for a lot less. Granted, $5,722 per week is a lot less than normal scale of $9,000-plus. But $70,000! Sure, grip and electric will gladly schlepp for a flat $50 a day so that the director won't have to "break down conditions" and work for less than scale. And don't forget to include that dressing room on location and to provide that personal assistant as called for in the Basic Agreement.

What's that, you say? The DGA has a low-budget method that lets you defer part of this money? Let's see if we understand this. For anything budgeted up to $1.8 million, all you have to pay is 50% of scale up front and 65% at "break even," if you ever get there. Well, okay. That's only $35,000. "What do you say, grip and electric, now we can pay you $75 a day (that's still flat; come on, get real) and buy a few cans of generic soda to supplement the tap water and the Kool Aid fruit punch. If you guys designate a driver, maybe we can even afford some wrap beer at the end of the week. No problemo, right?" Oh, but wait a minute, what about those other DGA people? The UPM (Unit Production Manager) who has to be on a "qualification list." What is that? A First AD (Assistant Director), a Key Second, we have to hire them, too? And they get a guaranteed prep period? At least the UPM doesn't get that, so he or she can start the day before we shoot. And they'll all work for 50% up front like the director. They can work any five out of seven days, just like the actors, but they get time-and-a-half on Saturday and a week's pay for "completion of assignment" at the end! That's not good. And what's this, overtime after fourteen hours for the First AD and after thirteen (!) for the Second? Maybe we can make a side deal on that last one, but lets add this up for an eighteen-day, three-week shoot. And don't forget that Production Fee and fringes. Start with $1,313 a week for the UPM; but we're only paying the Director of Photography $1,250. Add in the First, the Second, the fee and fringes—that makes over $12,000 for the First AD alone and $28,604 total with no prep on the UPM. That's also $37,000 deferred that we have to make quarterly reports on until doomsday, or the Directors Guild of America will take us to binding arbitration. "Hey grip and electric, sorry, back to $50 a day; but here, have some icy, refreshing Kool Aid, then back to work. Hurry up, 'cause if we go past fourteen hours, that guy rolling camera gets another one-half day's pay. That's 140 bucks plus fringe. We don't need a sandbag on that shiny board, just shoot it!"

Does the DGA really think you that should pay more than 10% of your half-a-million-dollar budget to its members up front? They probably never sat down and really figured it out. Do they know how many of their members are out of work? Maybe it's time for them to wake up and smell the day-old coffee at the DGA.

And while we're at it, how about a reality check over at the Screen Actors Guild. Sure, they raised their low-budget ceiling, and you can still pay the rate from the analogous period of the last contract. That's still $400 a day, for eight hours! Plus fringes. And they're on the clock from when they start putting on their make-up until they take off their wardrobe. We don't think that's going to go down as smooth as Kool Aid with grip and electric. What's that? We don't have to pay them for "hold" days? Great, we don't have to pay them for days when they don't actually work. What a deal. (Did we miss something here? Oh, that's not like the regular contract, where we do have to pay them for days they don't work. Well, in that case, we say again, what a deal!) Of course, those picture-deal actors on a weekly contract, they still get paid for "hold" days. Wait a minute! Now we have to hire "stand-ins" for $99 a day for eight hours. And extras for $65 a day for eight; and the fringe just went up to 12.8%. But those people spend most of their time sitting around talking and playing cards. The assistant directors have to shoo them out of the head of line at lunch time so the crew get some food. "Grip and electric, guys, wait, don't quit. We'll give you each a twentieth of a net point. If we can gross as much as *Much Ado About Nothing*, after we pay off the DGA deferments, that ought to be good for a few hundred more. Don't go! At least we didn't sign with Writers Guild."

The ironic thing about all this is that, unlike imagination, it really isn't funny. We won't talk much about the Writers Guild. Don't most of their members make the lease payments on their 500 Mercedes by artfully penning sitcoms and scintillating episodes of *Silk Stalkings*? Is that a union show? Who cares; it is alliteratively titled television trash of the sort most WGAw (small w for "West") members get paid scale plus fringe plus residuals to limn.

Like we said, we're not writers. But we respect creative people. That's people with talent, not attitude. Fortunately, there seem to be a lot of people with writing talent who either are not in the WGA or don't mind bending its rules. After all, a writer really is just a name, not a face on the screen or a presence on the set. If he or she will take a reasonable sum and, if necessary to avoid sanction by their peers, subscribe to the time-honored tradition of the pseudonym, it really is no problemo.

Of course, grip and electric have a union, too. Locals 80 and 728, respectively, of the International Alliance of Theatrical and Stage Employees. So how come they're not on your set making sure the Kool Aid is fresh? They had more than a reality check some time ago. They looked around and discovered that it was over. Most of their members were out of work, losing their benefits, and really pissed off. Can you tell these people not to break down conditions? Not likely. The IA is trying to make a comeback, buddying-up with Teamsters (more about them below), and trying to organize shows. "Here you go, grip and electric, read this card, have an election, sign up with us. Sure, there's a chance that the producers will just fire you all and bring in a new non-union crew; but there's a chance they won't. What's the budget? $700,000. Well, then, there are two chances they won't." Because "slim" and "none" don't hack it with grip and electric, the IA is not getting very far. They want to become what the Western Canadian IA has been for years, "we'll eat a bug to make a deal" kind of guys. For those of you who don't get the joke, "bug" is what they call the IA seal when it's placed in the end credits of a picture. (Sometimes you have to explain 'em. There was a time when IA projectionists would not screen prints that did not have the "bug" on them. Those days are also long past). But underneath the new line, the same old (operative word) business agents have the same old attitude. Afraid of the Teamsters? Worried that a bunch of goons with Irish and Italian names will descend on your set with lead pipes and baseball bats to wreak havoc on personnel and equipment? Don't believe everything you may have seen in *Hoffa*. (Danny De Vito, did he have Teamsters on the first picture he directed? He didn't?)

So what do you do when the IA or the Teamsters throw up a picket line, pull their members, and threaten to shut you down? Hopefully, you've kept a low profile appropriate to your micro-budget, and these folks will stick to the bigger fish. If not, you can ignore them, which usually works, or you can go for the real side deal.

These are not the side deals written in contract language by the unions and guilds which require signatures in ink or blood. These are side deals written in sand and sealed with a handshake. This is the information that you bought this book for, but before we get into it, a brief lecture.

The reason most of these guilds and unions have an attitude is because of a long history of real abuse by both the major studios and the independent producers. The major studios signed up long ago, and their productions are what keep the guilds and unions afloat. Sure, they work around the contracts with bogus "negative pickup" deals, which have them financing non-union productions while pretending to remain at arm's length. Their lots are not completely closed anymore, so that people who are not in the IA can actually work on a sound stage at Universal. But if you can afford to rent a sound stage at Universal, you're probably beyond five, ten, or twenty-five thousand per day, so give this book to someone who can really use it.

The problem is that today's independent producers, working in a market that is as tight as it ever was, facing distributors who, as we already noted, act toward film-makers like sharks around a bleeding swimmer (more on this later), are still facing rules designed to thwart the unscrupulous "no-pay artists" of generations past. If you are a no-pay artist, we wish you had not bought this book, and if we could, we would rip it out of your hands. If you are thinking about being a no-pay artist, remember that if you want to make more than one movie in Hollywood or any other town, good reputations are hard to build and easy to lose. Remember what we said about the WGA? Well, people who make deals and renege, who write bad checks, who say "so sue me" to hard-working talent and technicians, deserve to be regarded as pond scum, because if the cliché fits, they should wear it. Better yet, it should be tattooed to their foreheads.

It's because of no-pay people like this that SAG has such an unreasonable attitude. "Want to hire our members? Sign here. Not your phoney Delaware corporation, you, individual producer, sign here. Then sign this UCC-1 giving us a demand lien on your copyright. (Translation: You don't pay, we take the picture.) Then give us a cashier's check for at least 40% of your cast budget. More, if we don't like your smirk. If you pay the actors on time, we'll let you keep going. And when it's all done, everyone is paid, and all the pension, health, and welfare is received, eight weeks or so after you finish shooting, we'll give you back your deposit with a smidge of interest. You're making this picture for $350,000, you can't afford to post a bond, the actors are investing their salaries because they love the project. No, they're not. No signature and check, no deal. Get yourself some non-union actors who love the project. Try the local small theatres—people work there for free. If we find any of our people in front of your cameras, we'll pull them off, fine them, and put you on our list of bad boys and girls."

So how do you do it? How do you make that picture for $350,000 with those talented actors who love the script without getting them and yourself on the SAG bad list? We're taking you at your word that you love the project, too, and are not a crass exploiter, so read on.

If you are the low end of the 5/10/25, just cross off the DGA, the WGA, the IA, the Teamsters and consider those local theatres where non-SAG actors work for free. It will make your life a whole lot less complicated. Now let's assume, for whatever reason, that members of these unions and guilds are working on your picture and you need to make some sort of accommodations.

Option 1: If none of them care, conceal their identities. This is certainly not difficult for the WGA or the IA, with whom you are unlikely ever to come to terms, even at the high end of 5/10/25. As a matter of course on any independent production, all your shooting locations should be kept confidential. Not secret; you can't hide from a really determined business agent or guild rep, anyway. But you don't need to put yourself in the trades with those scores of other "Pictures in Preparation" that never actually start shooting. All that will get you, if you have an interesting title or a recognizable name in your cast, are (assuming you don't have a distributor) standard phone calls from low-level acquisitions people at various distribution companies; queries from hundreds of equipment vendors, purveyors of services, and out-of-work crew; and assorted grief. If you can live without this, don't list the project.

Unfortunately, if, for casting purposes, the script has gone to Breakdown Services, which distributes a synopsis and thumbnail descriptions of the parts to all the talent agencies at no cost, the trades and other interested parties will hunt you down. In this regard, pseudonyms are very useful from day one. They are *de rigueur* for WGA, DGA, and IA working outside the contract. This seems so simple, can it really work? Sure, as long as you remember what you are doing. One director, who must remain nameless but who worked on a series in the '50s that featured the talents of Warren Beatty and Florida Friebus, did a plethora of low-budget features without portfolio. He kept a low profile and only got found out because he started letting his name appear on crew lists as director rather than creative consultant.

This is all well and good for directors, writers, etc. But, unless they hide behind fright wigs and spectacles and alter their voices, the real identities of actors are there for all to see and hear. Besides, if their identity helps sell tickets and/or rent videos, concealing it might be a trifle counterproductive. Don't have that 40% for SAG? What do you do?

Option 2: Shoot first, pay later. This requires a really low profile and an actor willing to crapshoot, but it's not that hard. The examples coming later provide details on how to use this method, but the theory is simple. You tell SAG that you will be shooting on a given date. Four-

teen weeks of pre-production on a $400,000 budget? Why
not? If some rocket scientist of a rep at SAG actually questions this, you say something to the effect that most of
the people are working deferred, the office space is free,
and because the budget is so tight, you want to take a
lot of time to prepare in detail because you can't afford
problems when you actually shoot. Don't quote us exactly, because that rocket-scientist rep may have read this
book, too, but you get the idea. The signatory documents,
the pre-production cast list, 40% deposit, etc., are due two
weeks before principal photography begins. By now you
must have figured out that you actually prep for six, shoot
very discretely for four, and have been wrapped and the
actors all paid (key point) for two weeks before SAG expects to hear from you. Then what do you say?
"Whoopsie." "Whoopsie?" Yeah, that's the ticket. Does it
work? Maybe not more than once, but it works. You paid
the actors didn't you? That's the bottom line. What is SAG
going to say? "Tsk, tsk." You can live with that; your picture is in the can. What about that UCC-1? Do you owe
them money? No. Then don't worry about it.

Does this really work? It has before and it will again.
But it is a bit of a tightrope walk. Bad sense of balance?
Try Option 3, fringes only. You may recall that we alluded
to this earlier, and there are more details in the upcoming examples. Let's consider the abstract. How do the
guilds and unions know that their members are being
paid? If they suspect you, extreme measures may be imposed. Like SAG, the DGA wants a UCC-1 and monies
escrowed. But SAG doesn't actually pay the actors from
its security deposit, and the DGA escrow funds are not
sent to the guild. You pay the actors and any other guild
and union people, and you send the fringe to the pension, health, and welfare offices on the individual's behalf. You also send SAG copies of contracts containing
the rate of pay (likewise the DGA) and daily reports on
which actors work and for how long. This means that if

an actor is contracted for $10,000 a week (a round number for hypothetical purposes, not a suggested rate of pay), SAG expects to get $1,280 in fringes for every week worked. Unless SAG has some reason to suspect you, you don't actually have to send copies of the canceled paychecks. They go by the fringes; so if you pay the actor zero dollars but send in a fringe amount that matches the contract and the SAG Daily Time Report, then all is copacetic.

Using Leverage to the Max

The bottom line is always the same. If people love you and/or your project, if for some unknown reason they want to work with you no matter how little money you have, they will work for nothing. In theory, there is a difference between nothing and a deal for deferred pay and/or profit participation. At the 5/10/25 level, there is no practical difference. The examples that follow will illustrate how commitments to work for a price may vary. But assuming that the commitment you have is solid, then anything is possible. If your cast and crew are willing co-conspirators, there is no such thing as a union problem. What is more important is that, once you have a commitment from one or two people, it provides significant leverage for everyone else, as in, "Well, Arnold normally makes $15 million, but he's working for scale and net points on this. Maybe you could consider lowering your asking price a tad?" Or "Panavision gave us everything for a flat $11,000 for the run of the shoot. Maybe you could let us have that 750-amp tow plant that's just sitting on your lot for $350 a week?" The more people that actually climb aboard your low-budget express, the easier it is to fill those last couple of seats.

Remember what we said about finding the hook and dusting off your SAG card. Remember, too, what we said about feathers and fish eggs. You have two scripts on any

5/10/25 project: the one you hope to shoot and the one that guides your performance in wooing cast and crew.

For Instance

> Had the spirit of prophecy directed the birth of this production, it could not have brought it forth at a more seasonable juncture, or a more necessary time.
>
> Thomas Paine, *Common Sense*

We may already have given you some common sense, but enough of this theory. It's time for some practical examples.

Nightforce (1987) is a perfect example of how things can go completely and ridiculously awry. The plan was simple: Make a picture for $545,000 starring Linda Blair with enough shower scenes, automatic weapons, and deafening explosions to sell plenty of video cassettes. The now-defunct (and movies like this are part of the reason) Vestron was backing *Nightforce* under its Lightning Pictures subdivision, an aptly named entity where lightning struck often and always cost a lot of money to repair the damage. Lightning specialized in $250,000 direct-to-video cheapies, most of which were ground out in New York by the late, sometime-porn director Chuck Vincent. A Hollywood irony: The head of Lightning went on to become president of Lightstorm, director James (*Terminator*) Cameron's company, which produced *T2*, one of the most expensive pictures ever made. How he got that job is a real mystery. Maybe somebody confused the company names. One imagines an agent snapping his fingers at some flunky and saying, "Get me what's-his-name, the president of Light-something on the phone." It only takes a couple of misdirected, high-powered calls for the wrong concept to stick. Anyway, this guy and Cameron just got divorced over creative differences.

But back to the point. Rather than just cough up a measly 250 Gs, which at this point in the company's history was chump change for Vestron, Lightning would get low-budget filmmakers to run up hours of toll calls to their staff lawyers in Stamford, Connecticut, going over dozens of pages of boilerplate contracts that said essentially, "Vestron gives you this piece of paper promising to pay X dollars on delivery. You go to our bank, pay them some points and interest (that expenditure really shows up on the screen) to borrow the money, make the picture, be personally responsible for all cost overruns (i.e. your producer fees are held back until delivery), deliver it exactly as promised, and then we give you the money to pay off our bank. And by the way, you sign over copyright and we own the picture throughout the universe in perpetuity." What a great deal. With the promise of plenty of shots of tanks exploding, not to mention Linda Blair's bare breasts (try saying that fast five times), Star Cinema, the *Nightforce* production company, had gotten Lightning to sweeten the pot.

The principals of Star Cinema had previously turned out *Malibu High* and *The Great Skycopter Rescue*. In these earlier efforts, they had stretched their dollars in the usual ways, one of the most imaginative of which was their hands-on film courses. Star Cinema had actually charged people to take courses in Gripology and the fine art of Craft Service and, as an extra added bonus, had permitted people to try out their newly acquired skills on real features. Star Cinema actually got people to pay them for the privilege of working on a movie!

The strategy on *Nightforce* was more straightforward: low wages. After logging ninety-plus hours at $160 for a six-day week, a second assistant director might have noticed that his or her pay rate was a bit below the minimum permitted by statute. Star Cinema also signed Linda Blair and other SAG members to a variant form of personal service contracts. The stars assured them that, even if the Screen Actors Guild discovered them working on a non-signatory production, they would not withhold their services. They also contracted services with the various technical personnel. The special-effects man signed a contract guaranteeing to "provide" all the extensive scripted effects for a flat fee and to be responsible for any overruns. A movie ranch in the San Fernando Valley that rented out halftracks and old Sherman tanks would provide a discreet location on private property miles away from the Screen Actors Guild's Hollywood headquarters or anyone else's prying eyes.

Because this was a bank-financed picture, a completion bond was provided by a company tied in to the Lightning slate. Amazingly, the bond company accepted the Star Cinema contract concept. Not so amazingly, when SAG showed up on the set, the actors walked. When the hours stretched out and the technical costs piled up, many of the crew hit the silk. The bond company had to take over and finish the picture; and $300,000 later, they may have wondered if anyone got the license number of that runaway tank.

Stranger's Kiss (1984) is the right way to do it. Three guys who all worked on Bogdanovich's *They All Laughed,*—Blaine Novak, Doug Dilg, and Sean Ferrer— were just sitting around chewing the fat when a light bulb went on over their heads and somebody said, "Hey, let's all pool our talent and resources and make a movie. Where do we start? Let's rent an office. How about David O. Selznick's old dining room at then-Laird, now-Culver Studios?" Here's a film lot with a checkered history, and it became a supporting character in *Stranger's Kiss.* Thomas Ince, one of the first tycoons, built it before his mysterious attack of appendicitis on William Randolph Hearst's yacht (catch the apocryphal details in Anger's *Hollywood Babylon*), and it subsequently belonged to RKO, Selznick (the front mansion was his logo), Desilu, J.R. Laird (Denver oilman ultimately busted by IRS), Grant

Tinker, and now Sony Pictures. They've shot everything there from *King Kong* to *E.T.*, and it's still an open lot.

Anyway, one of the three musketeers was out catching some rays when a studio maintenance man walked by, complaining about how dead it was. Light bulb Number 2: Let's write a script and use the studio as background. These guys pulled together a script (borrowing some concepts from Stanley Kubrick's early work), a cast, and a crew in less than eight weeks. The British (non-DGA) director was looking to showcase his talent in an American production. And he had an actress named Victoria Tennant sharing his digs. Novak was a basketball buddy of Jack Nicholson's. Don't start shaking your head, because they never got Nicholson; his man, Sandy Bressler, wasn't about to let Jack work on an "experience" project. So they got Peter (before *E.T.*) Coyote instead. They had an upcoming production designer in J. Michael Riva (now Dick Donner's regular guy), a Russian émigré d.p. named Misha Suslov, Gato Barbieri on music, and experienced folks at all the major positions.

Michael White, producer of *My Dinner with Andre* and *Moonlighting* (the feature with Jeremy Irons, not the TV show) ponied up $150,000. There was no bond or contingency on this private money, so when that ran out, Victoria Tennant threw in $25,000 more. On that budget, the crew had to be 100% deferred; and all the cast except for two day players endorsed their checks back to the company. What the money went for was (1) film, fresh from Kodak with their standard 2% cash discount; (2) food, from Sushi King (?!) at $5 a head with the rest deferred; (3) power charges from Laird/Culver, with stages, equipment, etc., deferred; (4) extras at $5 per day with screen credit for all; and (5) sundry expendables from lumber to gels and rentals that could not be promoted for free.

This is one of those pictures where everyone owned a pro rata piece of the net profits. Unlike most of those pictures, people have actually gotten paid something on *Stranger's Kiss*—not much, but maybe 10% to 15% of their deferred salaries. You might figure that a pickup deal from Orion Classics would put these brash young guys over the top, but it was actually the worst thing that could have happened. Like Miramax did with countless independents, Orion tested it, then dumped it. It did make some coin in Europe, where Parisians queued up around the block, and shone on the festival circuit at Berlin and Deauville. The extras may have gotten stiffed when the casting company never doled out the money they got on their behalf; but on the whole, people who worked on this picture don't feel that they wasted their time and effort, which says more about its micro-budget success than its grosses.

CHAPTER THREE

> It does not matter which we take . . . for
> our illustration; the principle is obviously
> the same in all, and in fact applies equally
> to the production of a house, a statue, or
> any other complex.
>
> Aristotle, *Physics*

Whatever Happened to the B-Film?

It's time for a little bitching about "what happened to the low-budget movie?" There's always been a B-budget category, from the original Poverty Row studios, Monogram and PRC, to successor enterprises like Allied Artists and AIP. Even the major studios had their B-units, films they deemed less prestigious. The movies often had minor actors, shorter shooting schedules, and less-prestigious directors. But what they lacked in budget they made up for in intelligence and style.

And what classics were produced at this level of financing: thrillers of the hard-boiled school like *Gun Crazy, Detour, The Big Heat*; timeless science fiction epics like *Invaders from Mars, The Thing*; classy horror potboilers like *The House of Usher* and *The Masque of the Red Death*; message flicks set to music like *Easy Rider* and *Five Easy Pieces*.

Remember those titles? If you don't because you're too young or your mind is failing with premature senility, then head for your favorite video store, plunk down some loose change, and spend a night with some true

American classics—not *Gone with the Wind* or *The Sound of Music*, bloated, smarmy, big-budget whales. Watch instead the well-oiled, slick sharks of the movie sea, low-budget masterpieces. And then you ask yourself, "What happened?"

These films didn't need the business end of a ski pole in the eye socket every few minutes or a toothsome blonde flashing her breasts when the plot slowed down. If they had intelligence and wit behind them, they used it. Of course, they knew they had to aim at a mass audience, that they had to be racy and sensationalist. But was that the end-all and be-all of these films? We think not!

Once upon a time, there was a movie industry run by money-grubbing entrepreneurs who loved movies. Nowadays, the industry is run by money-grubbing Yuppies who want their MTV. In order to appeal to that testosterone-pumping young stud, who the pundits say is the only one going to the movies and dragging his date with him, filmmakers are churning out mega-budget comic-book films. And these comic-book films of the '80s, such as *Terminator* and *Robocop*, make a fortune, pushing the rest of the films up against the proverbial wall.

In the past, the big films took a smaller segment of the market, leaving room for a variety of movies. Of course, the potential film audience was much larger then. People of all ages went to the movies once or twice a week. Why was that? Was it because there was no MTV, no premium movie channels all showing the same film? No, the real reason is that the industry made a wide assortment of movies that appealed to a variety of groups—young, old; male, female; rich, poor; white, black, brown—not just that elusive hypertrophic young stud.

Is your movie going to be able to go up against mega-hits like *Ghostbusters* or *Teenage Mutant Ninja Turtles*? We don't think so. That's why we've been urging you to forget the exploitation route. The big boys have that sewn up. Try smart, salable ideas, with a little bit of sex. Try making a film filled with snappy dialogue and engaging characters, with a little bit of sex. Use as your model a film like Robert Rodriguez's *El Mariachi* (1993): spend $7,000 and end up with a multi-picture deal at Columbia.

Picking a Format: Choices, choices, choices!!!

> There is no material that exists for the production . . .
> Buddha

All right, you've sat through our diatribe on the decline of the B-movie. Either that or you've recycled those pages and we don't want to know how. You're probably saying, "C'mon, guys, get back to the technical stuff. What's my next move?" Like Aristotle said, "The principle is the same," but movies are the mother of all "other complexes." The particulars vary. And if the material you need doesn't exist, improvise.

Your next move is to figure out what format you're going to shoot in. Here are some of your options:

1. 70mm (65mm negative)
2. 35mm anamorphic
3. 35mm 3-perf
4. 35mm widescreen 4-perf
5. 16mm
6. Super-16mm
7. Super-8mm
8. 3/4-inch video
9. 1/2-inch video
10. 8mm video

There are two considerations when choosing your format: namely, what is your projected immediate market and what are your possible future markets? Are you planning on going directly for domestic and foreign video-cassette release and possible cable sales? Or do you want to try for theatrical distribution first, then later video and cable?

Let's dismiss Format 1. While 70mm is occasionally used for widescreen release prints, except for special processes like Imax and Showscan, no commercial film-makers have used it in over twenty years, since *Ryan's Daughter*, until Ron Howard dusted it off for *Far and Away*. This is a guy who started out holding hands with Andy Griffith on network television and directing *Eat My Dust* for Corman. Ron, shrink that head a little, babe. No wonder you've lost your hair. All that swelling around the follicles must have killed it. On 5, 10, and 25K a day, 70mm is not a consideration unless you're going to make a film about sunsets with no cast and crew, just you and an immense 70 camera. If you do decide to do that, though, at least give us co-story credit.

Film too pricey in any gauge? "What about shooting in video," you ask, "either in that old industry standby, 3/4-inch, or those newer, sleeker, cheaper formats like 1/2-inch and 8mm video?" Boy, you guys ask good questions. Yes, those formats will save you a lot of money on stock and processing. You can record every shot over and over again on the same piece of tape until the oxide wears off. And no processing. Then what's the downside?

What do you see shot on tape nowadays?: some sitcoms (not all); talk shows; variety and awards ceremonies; and, of course, the biggest feature-film user of tape, porno. Pornos are now mostly shot on videotape. With the boom in the home-video market over the last decade, porno producers saw their customers voting with their feet. Why venture into dark, dank adult theaters, where every man in the audience is wearing a raincoat (no matter what the weather), when you can sit in the cozy comfort of your own home and watch *Debbie Does Dallas XX* for the hundredth time? It's also cheaper—one to three dollars for a rental versus seven bucks for a theater ticket. So slowly but surely, porno producers got the message. Assuming you are over twenty-one, we and your local non-Blockbuster video store invite you to take a look at the result. Pornos on film were already cheap-looking. On tape, you could put all the star filters and digital effects you wanted on them, but pornos were and are a new high (low?) in cheap-looking.

We talked about expectations already, and when consumers attend a theater or rent a regular movie, they don't expect to see tape. With its compressed exposure range (the cause of that wonderful flaring), limited contrast, and desaturated chroma values, tape gives itself away subliminally to all but the most myopic of viewers. Feature films, whether made for the theaters, video, or cable—even Movies-Of-The-Week—are not shot on tape.

"You mean to say that most movies made for cable or for direct video-cassette release are shot on film?" Yes, Virginia, they are. Even though the producer has no expectation of a theatrical release, he/she knows that most video distributors want a classy product that looks as good as a theatrical film. And there is a major difference that any viewer can see between the look of a project shot on video and one shot on film.

Anyway, don't be shortsighted. You may *think* your only market is video release and cable. What if you find a theatrical distributor who just creams over your film, wants to give you a sizable sum for a theatrical release, and asks you to deliver a 35mm print to his office? (If you don't think this can happen, look at the list of titles from the '80s such as *El Norte*, made for public television, then successfully released in theaters.) Now you go back to your partners to tell them the good news, but there is one problem: no negative. And if you think a video-to-film transfer is going to convince anyone that this was shot on film, just look at *Norman, Is That You* (1976), if you can find it anywhere.

So we've narrowed you down to Formats 2 through 7. Ideally, you want to shoot in 4-perf 35mm widescreen, the industry standard. It has the highest resolution, definition, clarity, and color saturation. And utilizing short ends, which are the unexposed portions of longer rolls that many film stock houses sell at a discount, you might even be able to do this at the bottom end of our budget scheme.

Within 35mm you have two more options. "Oh, no, more choices," you scream. Don't despair. The first is anamorphic widescreen (an aspect ratio of 2.40 to 1 as opposed to the 1.85 to 1 of standard 35mm widescreen). Few films are shot in this format because equipment and lighting requirements typically make it costlier and more cumbersome. Some pictures like *Delusion* have used anamorphic effectively on a limited budget in well-lit exterior locations (in this case, Death Valley); but most low-budgeters should discard this option.

3-perforation 35mm is another interesting choice. It's fairly new, utilizing less of the normal 4-perf frame area and thereby creating 25% more running time on the same amount of stock. At one time, Lorimar was shooting many of its projects this way to save money. But soon they discovered its inherent disadvantages: First, you have to transfer it to 4-perf film in order to project it, which is costly, and secondly, filmmakers, when they discovered that they had 25% more of a cushion, just shot 25% more film.

One notch below in price and quality are 16mm and Super-16mm. 16mm is a completely respectable format. When blown up to 35mm for theatrical distribution, it gains grain but not enough to disturb the average viewer. And on video we defy you to tell the difference. A well-shot 16mm film looks as good as a well-shot 35mm film on video cassette or on most monitors, unless you're one of those people with high-definition TV. But who can afford those things, anyway? Some memorable films that were shot on 16 and released on 35 are *El Mariachi, Enchanted April, The Texas Chainsaw Massacre*, and *Return of the Secaucus 7*, a motley crew if ever there was one.

Super-16mm is a rarely used option that was promoted heavily a few years ago by independent filmmaking mags. Like Super-8mm, Super-16 uses more of the frame so that the image has more resolution when you transfer to 35. The most notable film shot in this format was *The Ballad of Gregorio Cortez* (1982). It was a fine film that looked good on the big screen but not noticeably better than any film shot in regular 16mm and blown up to 35. In addition, the equipment for Super-16mm is harder to come by and can be expensive to rent.

If you're scraping the bottom of the barrel, selling your blood to buy stock (and we sincerely hope you're not), there is the lowest option, lowest in more ways than one. Although Super-8mm enthusiasts are always promoting their beloved film stock with magazines, festivals, and awards ceremonies, it is a dying medium. It is getting harder and harder even to find equipment new or used, especially as most of the manufacturers have stopped producing it. Even the film schools like USC, which used to require their first film projects in Super-8, have moved over into video. Don't get us wrong. There are still labs and rental houses that handle Super-8, although they are far and few between. Luckily, for the moment, Kodak is still producing the stock and processing, although they keep threatening to drop the format.

The only film we are aware of that made the transition from Super-8mm to regular video-cassette release is *A Polish Vampire in Burbank* (1986). Although it was shot on Super-8, the filmmaker, Mark Pirro, spent a great deal of time and money in a video post-production house doctoring and mixing the film so that it would look like 16mm. For the most part, he succeeded.

No matter what your format decision, base it on your resources and on a realistic assessment of your potential markets. Be realistic, yet be hopeful.

Using Even More Leverage to the Max

Now that you have that award-winning script in hand, several thousand dollars burning a hole in your pocket, and a format securely chosen, what's next?

A good place to begin would be to study some other successful filmmakers who have risen from the muck to grab the brass ring of a multi-picture deal with a major studio. *El Mariachi*, as mentioned before, is a homegrown film made for a whopping $7,000 in cash, which so impressed the bigwigs at Columbia that they rushed to the door of 24-year-old filmmaker Robert Rodgriguez with bundles of cash and pages of contracts in hand.

What attracted these erstwhile lawyers and agents-turned-movie-execs to *El Mariachi*? Well, first, it was cheap, yet professionally made. The photography was crystal clear, the acting admirable, and the story action-packed yet filled with irony. Here was a filmmaker who could tell a smart story within a limited budget. Here was a director who wouldn't bring in bloated films that weighed the studio down with debt.

How did Rodriguez manage it? The stories are already becoming legend. Rodriguez checked himself into a research lab as a human guinea pig. As they probed and tested him, he wrote his script while earning half the budget of the film. While not all of us have the dedication to sell our bodies in order to make a film (nor do all of us have bodies good enough to sell), the lesson is still relevant. Raise the money when and wherever you can. Use your free time wisely.

There are a few other lessons to be learned in all this. One is about using your resources effectively; for micro-budgets, it's the only way to go. Survey your own assets and those of your friends and collaborators. What do you own that could be used on a film? Cars? Use them. A house or apartment? Use it as a location. No house or apartment? How about a mobile home? A flat-bed truck? A cellular phone? Clothes? Here's what Rodriguez has to say on the subject: "Before I even wrote the script, I sat down and listed our assets. We had a school bus, a pit bull, a motorcycle, two bars, and a ranch. So I wrote the script around these elements." We've had exactly the same experience, and while it may not give rein to your muse, it doesn't mean that the script will stink, either. Make that inventory now. Don't leave out a single item. Every prop you find for your film is one less rental. Every location you can secure without a fee is another saving.

While we're on the subject of locations, lots of locations can be had for free, even if you or your collaborators are not the proprietors. All you need is a little finesse. For example, let's say you need to shoot a scene at a college. It's a tender moment between a guy and a girl as they walk hand-in-hand across the verdant campus. What could be more romantic? Now, normally a college will charge you thousands just for a few days of shooting. But if you limit your crew size, three or four people plus the actors and you, you can pretty much shoot without a permit or interference. After all, most large colleges have their own film students shooting constantly on campus. How do they separate you from them? Same deal for city streets. Shoot on Melrose, use existing light, a limited crew, and the chances of a donut-eating official in blue asking for your permit are slight. If you do work without portfolio and get caught, remember that SAG card, play dumb. Pack up and go home. In the worst case, hostility can lead to handcuffs and a night in the calaboose.

Let us tell you a little salutary tale about a film we worked on a few years ago. It was one of those axe-in-the-head epics. More blood than brains, except what seeped out of shattered skulls. We needed a university for one of the nubile starlets (isn't there always a nubile starlet in these films?) to attend and meet her heavily ensanguined end. UCLA wanted $10,000, which was more than the location budget for the whole film. So we picked a Saturday, took our cameraman, a piece of aluminum foil, a soundman with a Nagra, and three actors and shot the entire day. We even got a Uni cop to do a walk-on.

So you've got your props and locations. What about equipment, film stock, processing, etc. Here's what Rodriguez says: "I borrowed an Arriflex 16s camera, a tape recorder, and two lamps. That's it." "Borrowed" is the key word here. Although Rodriguez only had $7,000 to spend, he managed to use his leverage to the max to supplement that sum? What leverage did he have? The same leverage you have. You're a moviemaker. You're in a glamorous profession and you have a creative, moneymaking project which will thrust you and everyone else connected with you into the shadow of the great god Oscar.

Maybe there's a dentist with a location you need who has a daughter who wants to be the next Madonna. You can find a small role for her, can't you? Maybe there's an equipment-rental company whose head honcho really likes your idea and will rent you the equipment you need in return for a sizable credit and deferred payment he knows he'll never see. Same deal with the processing lab or the film-stock distributor.

But don't get hung up on equipment. Lots of equipment does not a great film make. Look at Rodriguez. With his two lamps, Arri, and tape recorder, he conquered the movie world. Got a wheelchair, then you'll have some dolly moves in your film. Got a shoulder harness with a camera mount (they're for sale and rent everywhere for almost nothing), then you've got a steadicam.

Let's say that your budget is on the larger end. Do you know there are freelance camera people who come with their own equipment at discount rates? Some of these guys even have their own trucks outfitted with just enough lighting equipment to shoot a living room, if not a haunted mansion. And it's all at a set price for the duration of the shoot—no running back and forth between set and rental house for that missing barn door.

What if you've got the budget and you just can't resist building your dream set on a sound stage. Don't look to the studios for sound-stage rentals. There are a number of places with a single sound stage, which they rent inexpensively, sometimes throwing in cyclorama and an array of lights into the single rental price.

What about actors? Where do they come from? Obviously, not from heaven. Have you ever had dinner with one? More to the point, hasn't an actor ever brought dinner to your restaurant table? They can arrive from several venues depending on, once again, your budget. On a minuscule micro-budget, you may have to resort to friends who are actors and who believe enough in your project to work for deferred payment. Barring that, there are drama schools, some at universities and colleges, some privately run. There's also the ever-faithful *Dramalogue*. *Dramalogue* is read by every struggling actor carrying trays in every eatery in town. The ads are free as long as you're legit. Once you put the ad in, within a week you will be deluged with résumés, photos, and tapes.

And do make sure that you are legit. Actors' organizations and trade mags like *Dramalogue* have cracked down on the sleazoids who would use ads to get a date or, worse, pry some cash for "expenses" out of unsuspecting, young thesps. In Tinseltown, even legally legit can be morally marginal. How many people plunked down thousands in hard cash to have their picture in a big glossy magazine that most producers either round-filed or used as a doorstop? Because of the recent rash of misuse, publications like *Dramalogue* may check your phone and address to make sure it's valid or even ask for a letter of reference or a written guarantee of some sort. These are not difficult demands. An old professor who thought you were the new D.W. Griffith will do fine. Or a note on your letterhead describing your project and your shooting dates will also suffice. You should have letterhead anyway. The best way to impress those labs, rental houses, and actors you're approaching is with some nifty stationery. It's cheap. Find yourself someone with a laser printer and make it yourself.

If your budget is on the high end, you can make some better deals with more experienced actors, which might include signing with SAG. We talked about this in the last chapter and will revisit it in the next one. Maybe you can't quite stretch your checkbook enough to pay SAG scale, but you have some SAG actors interested. If, à la *Stranger's Kiss*, you can get them to feed their salaries back into the production and pay their benefits to SAG in return for points in the film, then you can even get De Niro. (Dream on, you say. Check Bob's credits and you'll find a recent low-budget enterprise listed there.) Many prestigious high-priced actors have worked for near to nothing in a project they admired or in a part which stretched their "instruments."

As an example, take the film *Diary of a Hitman* (1992). It's a low-budget thriller with minimal locations but high-priced acting. How did the director, Roy London, get stars with medium-to-high price tags—such as Sharon Stone, Sherilyn Fenn, and Forest Whitaker—to appear in his project? He was their drama coach once upon a time. He used his leverage to the max.

At some point, hopefully, you're going to finish shooting and be ready for post-production. Again, your budget will determine the facilities you use, whether it's a Moviola in your living room or your own air-conditioned suite in a post-production house. The living-room route is nothing to turn up your nose at. You can rent that Moviola, splicer, squawk box, etc., dirt cheap; and if it's housed in your home, there's no space-rental costs. As far as editing at a post-production facility, you can again wheel and deal. Use that script, maybe even some of your more impressive dailies to get some in-kind contributions. Free Moviola? Free splicing tape? Free room? Don't underestimate your abilities as a salesman. Just think of your film as if it were a new Saturn (the car, not the planet). It sells itself.

The Planning Never Ends

All these tips and tricks might as well be written on water if you don't take Henry King's advice about organization (see his golden words under "Organizing Principles"). "Who's Henry King?" you ask again. He started out in silent pictures in 1912, made one of the first deferred deals with Janet Gaynor on *State Fair* in the '30s, did a slew of pictures at Fox, and closed out his career with *Tender is the Night* in 1962. In short, he knew which was the business end of a camera for over fifty years, starting back when they were hand-cranked, so we thought his observation, obvious as it might be, would be pertinent.

Organization covers everything from script and storyboards when you start to spotting notes for the mix. There's a much-repeated story about Alfred Hitchcock's mania for preparedness, that he worked out his films shot for shot before anyone loaded a camera. He was so well-prepared that legend says he could turn his back on the set and know that things would still be going the way he wanted them. Now, we're not suggesting that you bring your Watchman to the set and ensconce yourself in a cozy corner for the duration. After all, someone might walk away with the equipment, or the actors.

Pre-planning is the *sine qua non* (Latin is so elegant) of any low-budget film. Detailed storyboards, complete schedules, and detailed line-item budgets will keep you on track. Waste is like entropy. Relax for an instant and there it is. When you know how much time and money you've spent and how much is left in your treasure chest, you can face problems, find alternatives, and make decisions that much faster and more effectively. In the labor-intensive environment of low-budget, in fact, at any budget level, prep time is the cheapest thing you have, so use as much as you want. Lack of preparation leads not just to lost shooting days and dwindling bank accounts but to low morale. And with unpaid troops, this can really be a killer. Time trickles away when no one is sure why that piece of equipment is at the Church location when it's supposed to be at the slaughterhouse. Wasted film stock results from the director not planning out shots and covering his or her butt with a lot of unnecessary singles. Some overruns in equipment, location, prop rentals, actor OT are inevitable. But after you've spent so many days and weeks saving a few dollars, a moment's carelessness that throws them all away can understandably drive a filmmaker to tears. Plan!! Plan!! Plan!! And then plan some more.

Robert Rodriguez shot most of his setups in one or two takes. How? He rehearsed his actors until they were ready. Why run stock through the camera when actors don't know their lines? Spend the weeks leading up to the start of production drilling your actors. Make sure they're good and they know what to do before you set them up in front of those burning lights.

Get yourself good assistants, from ADs to a script supervisor. Just from a continuity point of view, they have saved many a low-budget film by keeping track of "inconsequentials." It's not just, Does the actor have the same jacket on today as he had on yesterday when we shot this scene, or did we shoot the close-up of the hooker blowing a kiss to our alienated hero, or even which side of the screen did the mass murderer enter from in the last shot? It's reminding the low-budget director, "You said you thought this sequence was great in the over-shoulder shots; do we really need singles?"

One of the best filmmakers to mimic for economical

use of resources is the legendary Roger "I never lost a dime on a movie" Corman. Never one to waste a day of shooting, a stray prop, or an actor with a few days left on his contract, Corman repeatedly gets two films for the price of one and a half.

After finishing *The Raven* with Boris Karloff a few days early in 1962, he turned around and improvised a film with Karloff and some relative unknowns, like Jack Nicholson, in the sets used for the former film. Within a few days he had a second film in the can, *The Terror*. The fabled *Little Shop of Horrors* was a single weekend's work.

Corman gave Francis Ford Coppola one of his earliest breaks in this manner. Also in 1962, Corman was in Europe (busy guy!) filming *The Young Racers*. Again, he reached the finish line early. So off to Ireland he shipped actors and crew, all under the direction of the sound man—Coppola. The result was *Dementia 13*; and the rest is film history.

Today, the "old man" is still employing the very same methods. When Katt Shea Ruben was finishing her vampire film *Dance of the Damned* for Corman, in 1989, she discovered that there were a few days left on the production in the strip-joint sets. When Corman caught wind of this, he immediately commissioned her to begin another film on the same sets: *Stripped to Kill II*, written over the weekend and shot immediately before the crew had a chance to catch their breath.

As a final tale of how filmmakers can conserve their resources and then exploit them to the max, we present for your consideration the sleeper hit of 1979, *Phantasm.* This well-made little horror film was shot over a period of months, sometimes on weekends, sometimes with several shooting days in a row. The money came from wealthy friends of the director and never approached seven figures, despite some pretty elaborate effects.

The crew was gathered from starving, literally and figuratively, film students who would do anything—and we do mean anything—to work on a feature. They were all given contracts with deferred payment provisions. Now when any savvy film student (we hope there are some) hears the words "deferred payment," he or she knows that really means, "You'll never see any money, honey. But it's a great credit." But, believe it or not, this film paid off big. Most of the crew actually received checks in the mail years later. *Phantasm* became a big hit, making back many times its original cost. The $15,000,000 domestic gross reported by Avco Embassy, the film's distributor, created the largest ratio of cost to earnings ever. And this was before video-cassette sales and foreign income.

How come? Well, it followed the unwritten formulas that we've been discussing. The filmmakers picked a subject with a few locations. In fact, the house they used in the film acted as a barracks for the crew and an editing facility. Shoot, go to bed, then shoot some more. No worrying about anybody being late for the set this way. They also limited their cast. They used a young, unpaid crew; but most of all, they delivered on their promises. The film was watchable. It was released. It was successful, and everybody got a little cash, a little glory, and a lot of experience.

Completion—Partial or Full?

> Suppose now that an artisan brings some
> production to market. And he comes at a time
> when there is no one to barter with him.
> Is he to leave his calling and sit idle in the
> marketplace?
>
> Plato, *The Republic*

Remember back when we said that you had two choices going in: (1) spend all you have getting the picture in the can, or (2) get all the way to a finished picture. Sometimes you pick 2 and Number 1 still comes up. *El Norte* is a picture that ran out of money repeatedly, lost crew because they weren't getting paid or got bit by rats in the sewer set, shut down, and came back, re-wrote, re-cast, re-shot, and finally got done.

Let's say you've mixed all your tracks, you've edited your work print, and are ready to strike an answer print. You check your company's bank account and find out that the ink on the checks has turned red. Are you left hanging? Do you pack up your tents and slip off into the desert night? Hopefully not.

If you've got anything, from a work print and a mixed mag track to selected dailies in rough continuity, you have something to show for your time and money. These are tangible assets that you can exploit. Now's the time to start showing what you have to some potential investors, studio hotshots, distributors (video and theatrical, foreign and domestic). We've had this experience, too, unfortunately; and while it's not exactly the catbird seat, it's better than rolling boxcars. But remember the metaphor we've already invoked a couple of times involving distributors, sharks, and blood. Well, the blood along with the sweat, tears, and expended *dinero* is yours.

If you think that the shark analogy is wearing thin, a producer friend of ours has his own story about distributors. He was wandering the hotel corridors at the American Film Market carrying under his arm a video workprint with a temp dub (what must this have been like before video transfers?) and some crude fliers. One distributor popped it into his VHS, watched a few minutes, and made him a low-ball offer. He went away to think about it. On the next floor, he got another nibble and mentioned the offer he had. "You don't want to do business with that guy. You'll never see a dime. He's a crook." Down the hall, the same story. As he was in yet another hospitality suite, showing his reel and being told again that all the other guys were rip-off artists, a buyer noticed his movie on the TV screen. "Isn't this *Cheerleader Camp Massacre?*" the buyer asked. "Sure," said the AFM's only honest distributor, "Are you interested?" The buyer shook his head and pulled one of the crude fliers out his bag: "I was. I thought I'd already bought it from Rico Fittipaldi down the hall." We've forgotten the name of the only honest distributor, but according to our friend, he or she is easy to find. It's whomever you talk to last; and if you're not sure, just ask them.

Finding completion money can in many ways be the easiest part of the process if you are willing to be fleeced, to give away large chunks of your potential earnings to those who are "last in and first out." We used that term before, and if you're still not sure what it means, remember what it all comes down to: money. The last people to put money in are the first people to get money out. Plus fees plus interest plus whatever else they can extort from you in your vulnerable state. Still, it's better than never finishing the picture at all.

Before, you were selling your idea and your winning personality. Now you have something tangible. You may be able to seduce a distributor (not sexually, of course. Well, unless . . . no) or, better yet, get your Aunt Ruthie to part with some of the interest on those municipal bonds. Find yourself a cheap screening room. You don't need plush seats and a red carpet or the name Paramount on the door. There are a number of reasonably priced, one-theater screening houses. They have projectionists, a dual system, and a few seats. That's all you need.

CHAPTER FOUR

Now in postulating we are irritable and wordy.
If any little question arises about any of these ideas,
we are able to examine them fully. But drag us
to practice and you will find us miserably
shipwrecked.

Epictetus, *Discourses*

Budgeting, the Sequel

Rather than go back and forth between actual budgets, some of which probably contain confidential information (yes, we know that it may seem we've violated plenty of confidences already, but some things are sacred), we are going to use a hypothetical budget. This is a real budget, but in the phrase popularized by the late, great Jack Webb, "The names have been changed to protect the innocent." The numbers, too. And the title. (But if you think this title is silly, you should see the real one.) So what's left that's real? Everything and nothing. Real budgets are just numbers on a page. Real movies are something else again.

The Line

This is, we suppose, where the term "line producer" originated; although for a while it seemed as if the line(s) that counted most with those "above" it was on a mirror. The concept is simple. Above the line is talent: writer, producer, director, and actors. Below it is technical crew and equipment. Extras swing both ways, depending on the form, but are mostly below, despite what SAG would have you believe. Most budgets separate below into production, post-production, and a catchall of overhead items from insurance to offices. The ratio of total above to total below should range no more than ten points either side of 50:50. As the total budget diminishes and the cost of durable goods acquires more relative weight, the ratio should move toward 40:60. If it doesn't, it probably means that you're asking some semi-has-been thespian to grace your set for a few days and shorting the crew to pay for it. (Who says we don't respect actors?) This could be, like Arnold says, a "big mistake." Or, it could save your bacon.

Let's trip through the above-the-line, gathering free rosebuds where we may (no allusion to *Citizen Kane* or prop sleds). The script should cost nothing. If all the scripts in Southern California were suddenly thrown into the Pacific, the high tide would sends waves lapping against the Hollywood sign. A lot of these scripts belong underwater; but there are lots of half-decent ones as well. How do you find them? Take out an ad? Sure, if you're partial to avalanches. Agency dumpsters? Good concept, but messy. Ask your friends. If they don't have one, they will surely know someone who does. But lay out the budget parameters in advance so that people don't bother you with *T3*. Ads can work, but only if properly worded. And make sure you use a post-office box or the address of someone you secretly hate for submissions. Remember these principles: Unproduced screenwriters do not need money. They need to become produced screenwriters. They do not need to be producers. They need to be read but not seen. If you must pay them something, do not start with hundreds. Anything less than a very low four figures is more ridiculous than no money. Corman pays $2,500 to $10,000 (you work your way up to the latter amount by doing a lot of the former). Roger and his ilk will continue to be our yardstick for all things micro.

The producer may also be uncompensated in micro-budgets. Before we go any further, note that once the budget rises to the point where it requires a completion bond, everybody that can be fired should have a salary, otherwise what will the bond company use to pay the replacements if they have to take over and make whole-sale changes? At the micro level, line producers are a lot of froo-froo, just another hungry mouth waiting for lunch. Associate Producers—please don't make us laugh. You can give these credits out like green stamps if you want, but try to avoid too many people with the same last name in the main titles. On 25K a day, you can afford to hire a producer; but make sure it's one who has worked at this budget level before. Getting a "favor" from some fast-talk-ing huckster who's done "some line producing on Mov-ies-Of-The-Week," is not a favor. Someone who doesn't have a clue (i.e., no experience) in low- and micro-bud-get is worse than no one at all. Turn your back on some-one like this for a couple of moments and he or she may have made enough bad deals out of ignorance to totally blow your budget. Pay ranges from $5 to $25 thousand for the picture.

If you, Mr. or Ms. Filmmaker who bought this book, are not the director, and the writer is not the director, and the person putting up the money is not the director, then we would expect the director to have said "action" and "cut" before. It's safe to say that of all the reasons for which people direct micro- and low-budget films, mak-ing a big fee is not at the top of the list. Some directors, like the second half of Shapiro/Glickenhaus, are part of the company. Some have worked in some other capac-ity on movies with larger budgets and want to cross over. One might expect a disproportionate number of first tim-ers in micro- and low-budget, but people such as the heretofore mentioned Fred Olen Ray or the Corman regulars like Jim Wynorski just keep coming back for more. $5K to $25K for the picture but usually around 2.5% (and never more than 5%!) of the total budget.

Actors—you can throw out the rule book here. SAG actors require scale plus 10% for those with agents or, if you make an unofficial side deal, at least fringes. Scale increases for actors and extras according to the contract period, but can always be obtained by calling SAG. For side deals other than 100% deferred, cash is always good; but a word of warning about those. There are not only union fringes but government fringes as well. You say that you don't expect to be nominated for the Supreme Court any time soon and you don't pay social security on money to your Salvadoran child-care professional, either? Well, those who provide a service, such as a person to whose home you bring a child, are not employees, no more than the people who rent you cameras, sell you film, or cater meals. Those whom you pay to report to a location and work under the supervision of others *are* employees; and unless they have loan-out corporations, not just Federal Employer I.D. (a.k.a. 95 numbers), you are legally required to pay government fringes on them. Will the IRS come knocking at your door if you don't? Not very likely. You can also look the other way if people choose to commit fraud and continue to draw unemployment benefits while you pay them in cash; and there is not much likelihood, for you, of being busted. *But* if you are busted, it can be big time. And you could be busted.

To put it in perspective, micro-budgeteers often can't afford negative insurance—and it's a lot likelier that the lab will ruin your film than the government will come nosing around. But either event could be catastrophic. If you form a corporation for a single picture, a one-shot deal and then it disappears, you can get away with a lot. Unless there is a compelling reason not to—e.g., you are tapped out and cannot pay an accountant to come in and do it—do not compound your liabilities by failing to file

1099-MISC forms on all those who are paid more than $600.

Back to the actors, who in non-SAG micros typically earn from zero to seventy-five dollars per day—do not make sweetheart deals with the untrustworthy, i.e., loose-lipped. Actors have a lot of time between takes to stand around and talk to each other, and money is a subject close to their hearts. "Favored nations" is great concept that can give you a lot of deal-making leverage. If you can roll that first semi-name in at scale, you can attack any agen,t no matter how supercilious, from a position of aesthetic superiority and scoff at their crass commercialism. It only works about half the time, but how big a cast do you need? Keep in mind also that SAG actors working for "fringes only" can cause you grief with a single anonymous phone call. Treat them well, even after they are finished in the picture, even after you've wrapped. Don't call any actor a jerk until you've got your deposit back from SAG. Even non-SAG actors can cause grief. If you suddenly piss them off and they won't show up for a final scene, it can leave a big hole in your movie. Remember, people working for free don't lose a dime when they decide to quit.

Time to go below-the-line, where rates vary ever more widely. The bottom line for labor is always either 100% deferred or plain no money ever—just the experience, which is reward enough for the star struck and the reel builders. Ironically, none of the government fringe and tax-reporting problems that plague the cash deal trouble the 100% deferred or the forever freebie. If you've got less than $100,000 and you're shooting in 35mm, most, if not all, of your labor will be lucky to get food and some gas money. If there are salaries, they can start at $50 per week. Given minimum-wage statutes, there is no way to pay this amount legitimately. The solution is to call it something other than wages, which would not be hard for most folks to believe, such as a car allowance.

Why not use this for any amount, you say, even $500 or $1,000 per week? Because if a government agency did check you out later, that would be hard to believe. At the next level of micro, $25 to $50 per day is normal. That is still flat and still likely to be below minimum wage, and most crew working for this sum will probably want cash, i.e., no withholding and fringes. If you can afford the fringe, the only reasonable way to pay a salary is to use a payroll service, which becomes the employer of record. Service charges vary from .25% of the amount paid to $10 per check; but the alternative will cause your likely-to-be-underpaid accountant to reach for the Mylanta and invite the hassle of unemployment claim processing, forwarding withholdings, and W-2 filing later on. Unlike 1099-MISC reporting, W-2s are due on any amount, no matter how small (those of you who have gotten residuals for less than five bucks know this already), and are certainly not optional.

At the high end of our 5/10/25 range, some people, such as the director of photography, may actually make more than $1,000 per week. When you have this option, structure your deals so that you are paying minimum wage, and any amount over that represents a minimum guarantee against overtime. Why? Well, in California and other states, when disputes are taken to the Labor Board, the assumption is that, unless otherwise stated, the agreed-upon daily or weekly amounts are for eight and forty hours, respectively. The base hourly is derived from this, and overtime is payable thereafter. This can permit a couple of disgruntled crew people to reach deeply into your pocket long after the fact. If they are doing this because you haven't paid them what you promised and you don't have a really good excuse, such as (minimally), "I'm sorry, guys, we ran out of money, I can't finish the picture and I can't pay you," then we're on the disgruntled crew's side. Don't take advantage of the grunts. Sooner or later, if your body doesn't catch a sandbag, your reputation will.

We talked about "favored nations" for actors, but the same works for crew. Ideally, whatever you budget for and actually offer one department head should be the same for all the others, i.e., $1,200 a week for the gaffer should mean $1,200 a week for the analogous job of key grip. Again, as with actors, if you can land an experienced department head at lower than the normal rate, you can use that fact as leverage. It's not just a matter of saying, "Joe's going to gaffe the show for $150 a day"; but implicit in your deal with Joe is that you wouldn't pay more to johnny-come-latelies. "Last in, first out" may be the only recourse in money raising; but in setting the crew, favored nations should always apply. If you say to a prospective key grip that the gaffer is already aboard for a particular amount, so you can't pay more, it had better be true. Just like actors between scenes, crew people have been known to compare notes.

The script can help or hinder in crew deals. If your script is good *and* appropriate to your budget, you won't have to draw good technicians a map. Everyone wants to do good work (everyone is building a reel it seems, even craft service people). Give them an opportunity, and they won't mind taking little or nothing for a few weeks. If the script asks the impossible, then only the blind or foolish will be interested at any price. If you could get Harrison Ford to work for scale, then you might be able to make *The Fugitive* on a low budget—but not unless you lost the train wreck. What this means is that responsible department heads may care less about their salary than their budget: the amount available to pay their crew and acquire materials to do their part in filming the script as written.

Equipment is another matter. We don't mean that there's no Labor Board for equipment. Unpaid vendors have a different kind of recourse, from lawsuits to badmouthing, none of which should be taken lightly.

Whatever deal you make for equipment is the deal you should honor. This does not mean that you should lie down and invite folks to treat you like a rug. Vendors break deals when they fail to deliver or deliver incorrect or inferior material, when they claim loss or damage that isn't accurate, when they add charges not previously agreed to. What should underlie any negotiation or re-negotiation are all the factors we've been discussing from leverage to reputations.

As with salaries, the range of rental prices is broad, but it seldom drops to zero. Sure, we've all heard stories about cameras being promoted from Panavision—and they regularly are for showcase shorts by AFI students. More commercial ventures can get major reductions from the rate sheet, but free is very tough. How big a break? How about a Panaflex Gold package with prime lenses and zoom, batteries, mags, sticks, Sachler head, all of it for $1,600 a week? Weekly rates are often expressed in terms of a daily rate sheet, e.g,. a one-day week is five days (or six or seven) for the price of one. $1,600 is less than a 1/2-day week. These, by the way, are real deals but strictly no quote. Don't expect to fax a copy of this page to someone at Panavision and get the same deal.

If you can't afford Panavision at any price, there are Arri BL packages that include a truck, grip, electric, and generator for $2,000 per week. No, these are not new HMIs and a Fisher dolly, but they do work. If your budget is really micro and you want to shoot 35mm, you must either get full or partially deferred deals on the equipment, which may be easier than you think when things are slow. Remember, equipment sitting on a warehouse shelf is earning nothing. If you only need it for a week or a succession of weekends and are willing to "fly standby" (and provide an insurance binder), any money is more than none, and even a deferred deal that promises "maybe money later" is better than no money for certain. There is a vast realm between Super-8 and Super-

Panavision 70; but at the high end of 5/10/25, the total weekly outlay for equipment (camera, grip, electric, generator, and production van) should not exceed $10,000.

Expendables are a slightly different approach. It is one thing to convince a rental company that has equipment just sitting around waiting for dust or rust to land on it. They give it to you, make a few dollars, it comes back. It's quite another to talk them out of expendables. You cut up a roll of gel, use up a can of dulling spray, or eat a sandwich and it's gone forever. Same thing for lumber, gasoline, or rolls of tape—the list goes on. So how do you get a bargain on these?

As you may well imagine, the number-one expendable is film; but there are a lot of alternatives. We've already talked about choices based on format; price is another factor. That fresh 35mm stock from Kodak is forty-four cents per foot. Fuji and Agfa stock can be had for around 10% less than that, and both companies can be approached about deeper discounts or partial deferments. There are also raw stock exchanges such as Dr. Rawstock and Studio Film and Tape in Hollywood. For unopened cans of previously purchased stock, the price dips to thirty-seven or thirty-eight cents. Re-canned full loads (i.e., film that had been loaded into magazines but never actually threaded into the camera) are one or two cents less. Long and short ends, the odd-length remnants of rolls that are broken off and recanned, vary in price depending on length. Obviously, a minute-long, 100-foot load is less useful than 950 feet, but it's probably five to ten cents less, maybe as little as fifteen or twenty cents per foot.

The other way to save on pre-owned raw stock is to cut out the middle man. Raw stock exchanges find film by calling the pictures listed in the trades and offering to buy their leftover film. You can do the same. You may even stumble onto a show that has so little film left over that it's hardly worth the bother of selling and will let you have it for nothing. (We've never gotten film for free, but we have given it away. The least we've paid is four cents a foot.)

Buying direct works for pretty much all expendables. When a picture wraps, leftover materials are either thrown away and/or stored by someone on the show. Typically, gaffers hold on to partially used rolls of gel and photoflood globes, costumers keep items of wardrobe, camera assistants keep short ends, etc. However, even five cents on the dollar may be sufficiently appealing to a producer or production manager to send those items to your "warehouse" instead. This is especially useful if you would like to build sets but can't afford to do so from scratch. We know several low-budget filmmakers who regularly use art directors and prop men with extensive stores of materials. The ideal is to catch someone just wrapping a pricey commercial or music video who can divert thousands of dollars worth of lumber destined for the dumpster into your hands.

Dumpsters may not be a great source for scripts, but they can yield (figuratively, at least, as we're recommending finding the stuff before it's gotten trashed) more than lumber. Anything, in fact, except exposed film, from props to prosthetics can be recycled. Even exposed film can be used as fill by editorial.

Before we tackle editorial and the rest of post-production, let's close out the shooting process. You are unlikely to use the sound stage or warehouse option; but, if you do have numerous scenes scripted for a complex location, that is something you might want to consider. Some examples of these, like restaurants or nightclubs, are readily available during off-hours and come already dressed and propped. In Los Angeles, even jails and police stations are maintained for shooting at the former city facilities in Lincoln Heights and Venice. Some studios, such as GMT in Culver City, have standing sets such as prisons and courthouses for rent. (Before you run down and book your day in court, a word of warning about GMT and other such venues: GMT reputedly stands for Great and Mighty Things, but according to several producer friends, GMT's practices fall far short of Christian ideals. Be wary of those vendors who insist on large deposits, for when undiscussed fees or suspiciously large loss and damage charges show up on the final accounting, the filmmaker anxiously awaiting a refund has very little leverage.)

Even if you are not using stages or warehouses, many practical locations will require build-outs and/or dressing; and the same strategies for raw lumber to finished items will apply. Locations are one of the most complex budgeting issues. This is one category in which the abundance of filming in Los Angeles works against the low-budget filmmaker, as property owners are aware of the substantial fees that major features and network television shoots are usually willing to pay. Few residents of the metropolitan area have traveled around for any amount of time without stumbling over an array of trucks and equipment sprawled over the city streets, indicating location filming.

We've already talked to some extent about locations and how to operate discretely without permits and agreements. This is something that should not be overdone. Basically, even if you are shooting on private property with the owner's permission, unless that area happens to be zoned for manufacturing, you must have permits and, if mandated, police and fire personnel. Not only are these people expensive, but, for a low- or no-pay crew, watching these uniformed professionals sit around all day eating donuts while the crew break their humps is very bad for morale. Police may usually be dis-invited if you are firmly on private land, but those ever-vigilant fire fighters may have to be there to prevent a stray match or a spark from a generator from igniting the landscape. How can you avoid them? If there is a legitimate safety issue, working in areas with solvents or in a National Forest during fire season, it is not recommended that you avoid them. Find another location instead. If the only reason for police or fire is purely bureaucratic, don't tell the bureaucrats. If you are in Los Angeles, where runaway production to hospitable cities and towns out of California is a sensitive issue, you may be able to use your lack of money but desire to abide by the law as leverage in getting permit fees and police and fire requirements waived. This is much harder to do in the popular smaller municipalities such as Beverly Hills and Santa Monica. You can designate as many locations as you want on a single L.A. permit for $150, but if your budget cannot afford even minimal fees, don't take a full production retinue along when you try to steal a location.

Food is also a location line item; and while you may be able to get people to work without pay, very few will toil without food. Catered meals can be paid for by the head. Trucks with kitchens are more expensive than vans arriving with chafing dishes, but both run between $10 and $17, sometimes plus salary for cook and driver (on union shows these are Teamster categories). The enterprising Penny Cooper, a large woman with a large family and a large car, caters out of the trunk of her old Cadillac for $7 a head. The only way to beat this price is box lunches. If you are only shooting on weekends, that and the occasional foray to McDonald's can work. On five- or six-day weeks, box lunches get old very quickly. We joked a lot about Kool Aid, generic soda, and other Craft Service alternatives. Water and coffee are indispensable. Whatever else you can afford, it's better to have a few quality items than a lot of junk. There's nothing like reaching into a cooler and coming up with a can of Iris to depress a crew member.

Transportation is the last production category. It's unlikely that you'll be able to afford Teamsters anywhere in the 5, 10, or 25 range, which is reason number 399 for keeping a low profile. If you can't hire Teamsters, you may still want to rent equipment from them. From station wagons to honeywagons, Teamster rolling stock is usually well maintained and less likely to be threatened by unemployed members of the international brotherhood. All this and the prices are reasonable.

This is a natural segue to the most significant category in Overhead, which is Insurance. In the last few years, not only does everyone from the smallest vendor to the largest city want to see proof of coverage, they all want to be named additional insured. A full insurance package breaks down into several sub-categories: (1) Negative and faulty stock, covering lab error, bad film or sound tapes, and, if you stretch it, scratches caused by human or mechanical malfunction; (2) Cast insurance against death or incapacity (normal is five leads and the director); (3) General Liability, against accidents with non-combatants; (4) Property, covering all rented equipment; (5) Workmen's Compensation; and (6) Errors and Omissions. Prices vary depending on policy limits, value of the items covered, and deductibles, but the norm is between 1.5% and 3% of the total budget. As you may have guessed, when you rub up against minimum premiums with micro-budgets, the percentage can be even higher.

Insurance is a necessary evil and, as such, is hard to circumvent completely. Although they prefer not to, some rental houses will let you buy coverage from them, at added cost of course. No city, however, will knowingly permit you to operate on its streets without its name being on a liability binder for at least $1 million and often $2 or $3 million. There is no economical way to pick this coverage up by the hour, day, or week.

Cast insurance is probably the least necessary, and most micro-budgets skip it entirely. Just make sure you cast people in good health and pray they don't turn an ankle on the steps of a honeywagon. Do you really need negative insurance? No; but if the lab makes a mistake and ruins a roll of film, they'll just say, "Oops," and hand you a fresh 1,000 feet. They won't charge you for the replacement stock, but they won't pay to send your cast and crew out to re-expose it, either. You can skip this entirely or go for a very high deductible that gives cheap coverage against total catastrophe. If you don't have liability coverage, there are a lot of places you won't shoot and you will be liable. (More about this below under Legal.) But a really micro-budget may mean just that. Assuming that you pick up property coverage as needed from vendors, we've left the two thorniest for last.

We talked about Federal and State withholdings and payroll services earlier in this chapter. But whether you pay your crew or not, whether they are employees for Federal and State tax purposes or you pretend they are contract labor, cast and crew are your employees for purposes of Workmen's Compensation. This coverage is legally required. In California and most other states, you can buy it directly from a State Fund for a minimum annual premium of around $1,600 against around 4% of the total payroll. Since payroll services are the employers of record, you can add their Workmen's Comp coverage, usually for a lower percentage than direct from the State Fund and with no minimum premium. If you don't have Workmen's Comp and someone is injured, see our comments under liability above.

Although almost all distributors absolutely require it before they will release a feature, there is a much simpler solution to Errors and Omissions coverage, which protects against inadvertent invasion of other parties' copyrights, invasion of privacy, etc. E&O premiums are not negotiable and range from $8,500 for one year to $12,000 for three; but you can buy it after the fact. The risk here is the concept of "inadvertent errors and omissions." Buying it after the fact is one thing; making a claim is another. Most carriers, suspicious types that they are, will assume that you bought coverage after you discovered an inadvertent error or omission, in which case, if a claim does come up, they'll probably tell you that you aren't covered for it. Still, these "shoot first, pay later" policies will satisfy distributors, and that, after all, is the point.

A final note on E&O with regard to photo releases: Most micro-budget filmmakers are aware that they should acquire photo releases, i.e., permission to reproduce the likeness of a person, place, or thing. Many forget that places and things have privacy rights just like people. Hence, before a work of art under copyright can be photographed hanging on a wall in the background, permission to reproduce it should be obtained. Obviously, common sense should prevail here. A Picasso calendar hanging on the wall should not be cause for concern. For the truly paranoid, most prop houses offer a variety of materials that are already cleared through blanket releases or because they are public domain. Privacy laws have a flip-side, which can save you a lot of grief. Before you send a harried production assistant scurrying after passersby for releases, remember that any person, place, or thing that is visible from a public thoroughfare (street, sidewalk, etc.) has implicitly surrendered his, her, or its right to privacy and can be photographed and/or sound recorded without permission.

Fixing It in Post

In general, editorial begins with two basic options: cutting on film or tape. Most of the high-end video systems for editing are digital. Whether film information is transferred to laser or hard disk, the speed and versatility of these systems is astounding. Cutting with a computer is like word-processing a film. But, just as some writers won't give up their old Selectrics, there are plenty of editors still working with Kems. For that matter, David Lean cut his last feature in 1984 on a Moviola. That may be a little like using a vintage Smith-Corona manual machine, but it can get the job done. Obviously, Avid, Ediflex, and D-vision are not brand names that the micro- or low-budget filmmakers can afford. But there are older, off-line systems (particularly the 3/4 machines using Convergence controllers, which are not good for cutting frame-accurate video but fine for film "work prints") that can be rented for the same or less than a Kem.

Many commercials, music videos, and even episodes of network television, which are never destined to be projected on screen, are transferred to tape directly from negative and cut using standard off-line and on-line methods. If your feature is strictly made for video, this could also make sense for you. Our assumption has been that even micro-budgeteers want to make a movie to be shown in a theater, hopefully at other than the cast-and-crew screening. This means that the negative must ultimately be conformed to the video cut. There are two ways to do this. The usual and costlier method is to print and sync up dailies on film, then transfer to video. After the picture is locked, the work print is conformed.

Mixing offers the same choice between film and video. The workprint can be the used to build tracks for a film or sprocket mix. Alternatively, this print can be retransferred to video for sound work interlocked with 24-track, 2-inch tape. A third option available at a few facilities is to interlock the film workprint with the 24-track machines. As little as seven years ago, mixing on video was highly unusual, and TAV was the only game in town. Now there are more than a score of facilities in Los Angeles that mix on 2-inch. Not only is it much easier to build tracks, but the shunt time saved, the few moments required for machines to reset before a second mixing pass is made, is so much shorter that the time saved video machines locked by time code rather than film machines physically held in mechanical sync by the sprockets on the workprint and mag film, can add up to several hours a day. Even if you're paying a lot less than $650 an hour at Todd A-O/Glen Glenn (who would give their child this name?), it saves not just cash but some of the emotional exhaustion that comes from waiting for resets. Even more significant, sound editing does not require the phalanx of high-priced editors and assistants, who traditionally would spend weeks building all the effects onto a dozen or more sound reels for each reel of picture, consuming vast quantities of mag stock and fill and requiring a mix facility that could drive a score of "dummies" loaded up with bulky reels of film. Video facilities are not only smaller, faster, cleaner, and quieter but astonishingly versatile. In slightly more time than it used to take to merely spot effects, they can actually be laid in. Even we were astonished when we visited a producer friend at a small facility in Hollywood. While he and the director were laying in source music, they decided that they wanted the sound of a jukebox changing records. From his keyboard console, the editor accessed a sound library stored on a huge hard disk and offered them twenty-seven choices. Seconds later they were listening to them in synch with picture. As visitors, our astonishment turned to relief when they picked number four and didn't take the five minutes to hear the others. Unless your budget is so micro that you must forego all transfers and use a rudimentary mix with limited music and effects, you should assume that your post-production sound will be on video. Package prices vary from as little as $7,500 (for transfers, music and effects editing, and mix) to over six figures. All packages are based on hourly rates, and if you fail to negotiate a flat fee, you may find overtime charges added on to the final payment.

    The only way that a video cut can be cost effective at the higher end of the 5/10/25 scale is *not* to make a work print. Yes, we know, you want to end up with an answer print on film. The procedure is a 3/4- or 1/2-inch video from the negative and your 1/4-inch sound tape that has two windows: the video time code and the edge numbers from your negative. Without getting too technical, these transfers cannot simply print every fourth frame twice to turn 24 frames per second of film into 30 frames per second of video. They must use a 3/2 pull-down in which the 24 frames of film are alternately printed 3 times and 2 times over the 60 video fields. Yes, video does have only 30 frames, but each has 2 fields. Unlike Europe, where both film and video run at 25 frames and such mixed-media work is a whole lot easier, 3/2 printing, which uses 12 frames times 3 (36) plus 12 times 2 (24) to turn 24 (12 + 12) into 60 (36 + 24) every second, is the "easiest" way to get from film to video in the United States. Aren't you glad we didn't get too technical?

Transferring to video at 250 to 300 dollars is probably a bit cheaper than making a workprint. The advantages are editorial speed and a pared down work area analogous to the differences between sprocket and 24-track sound work. A single person can edit and log video without assistants or apprentices. But there are many disadvantages. You don't see film dailies, which can make a director of photography very unhappy. It's not just color values that change but a scene that looks perfectly sharp on a television screen may be soft when projected on a theater screen. If you don't find that out until the answer print, you'll have to live with it. Video sound is even worse. The sound package usually includes the transfer of all the production sound again onto the 24-track; as with the picture, there may be defects that were not noticeable in video. Of course, sound problems can be fixed with ADR and equalization—that's what sound post is for. But the last problem with video cutting is the thorniest: conforming. Without a workprint, the only way to conform is to make a list of cuts from the edge number window, and the only thing to cut is the negative. Sound risky? It is. One mis-cut can cost you your only good take. There are negative cutters who specialize in this kind of cutting from a paper list (those who don't will likely refuse to do it), but they take longer, charge more, and still make occasional mistakes. Of course, the worse mistake we've personally experienced was ten years ago when someone misread the edge number on a workprint and cut the only take of a scene right in the middle.

If you are working on a micro-budget, you've got enough to worry about without taking the added risk of a video cut. Besides, if your editorial staff is, like your crew, working for short money or wholly deferred, cutting on film and mixing on tape will be the cheapest way to go. As with production, equipment and expendables needed for the editorial process can be had for less than book rate. Moreover, while it's hard to get any significant discount on film-to-tape transfer, as most facilities already work around the clock to fill orders from television shows and music videos, you may be able to get significant discounts on workprints. Either way, you have to process the negative, which normally costs from twelve to twenty cents per foot. Printing (which includes the stock needed for the workprint) ranges from sixteen to twenty-six cents. As always, rates are negotiable. Book rate at Deluxe is forty-four cents, but you can shave a dime off that. Discount at Fotokem is twenty-nine cents; rock bottom is twenty-six. At Image Transform and a few other labs, you can process and print for under twenty cents a foot; it is very hard to get processing only for under a dime. Obviously, if the labor is cheap, cutting on film will take longer but cost less.

It may seem strange to some to find Music widely separated from the "talent" above the line. Important as it may be to the finished film, on a budget form, the music account resides with the rest of the post. We're not much given to understatement, but that's what were doing when we say that there must be hundreds of composers out there falling all over themselves for an opportunity to write a score for a feature film. If these people have

the slightest inkling that you exist and might be recep-
tive, they will inundate you with demo cassettes. (On the
plus side, the abundance of audio and video samplers
that you may receive guarantees that, with those record-
protect tabs covered over, you will never need to buy
blank tape again.)

Once you understand that you won't be getting Jerry
Goldsmith or James Horner (would you want them anyway?), what do you budget for music? While composers
will work for 100% deferred, most musicians won't; so if
you want an orchestral score, that will not be free. Normally, composers accept a package price for a finished
score and hire contractors to book the sessions and players. Even using non-AFM musicians (or members without portfolio) in the U.S. and paying the composer nothing up front, an orchestral score will run at least $20,000.
What you have to decide is, even if you can tell the difference between real instruments and their synthesized
sounds, will most of your audience? Give an electronic
wizard with some musical talent, whose den is packed
with Macs and midis, a chance with a time-coded 1/2-inch
video of your picture and he or she will give you back
an astonishing, digitally mastered underscore. The presence of those folks, who often make a good living sweet-
ening commercial jingles or programming computers for
major studio sessions and really want a feature credit,
means that you can get all your music for virtually nothing. And whereas the price of orchestral scores increase
with the number of players, cues, and sessions, digital
scores are unaffected by these variables.

Original songs can be had for the same low price.
There are hundreds of eager tunesmiths out there who
are building résumés and will let you have their slickly
recorded demos at no cost. Scores more, who own, manage, or otherwise have access to recording studios, will
write you songs to order at no charge. If you have some
money and want to keep it simple, you can clear a dozen

pieces for a few thousand dollars through music super-
visors and/or stock libraries.

"Clearing" songs means obtaining two licenses: a
master use license from those who own the individual
recording and a mechanical license from the publishers
and/or copyright owners of the actual song. As the lic-
ensees are typically responsible for any royalties or residuals out of their fees, the hardest part of this is nego-
tiating the price. The mechanical alone permits you to
record you own version of the song. But unlike the recording the industry, where mechanical minimums are set
by statute and you can do anyone from to George "Bad
Boy of Classical Music" Antheil to Zappa for pennies,
"synchronization" rights for motion pictures vary according to publisher. And, no matter how low-budget you are,
some won't give you any break. The bottom line is don't
plan on clearing the Stones doing "Satisfaction" for a few
hundred bucks. Finally, don't believe those tall tales about
getting some record company to give you an album advance that pays for a whole lot of classics. You can get
an underscore and new or public-domain songs for next
to nothing. Pop some cassettes into your car player while
driving to and from the set and discover some new talent. Music is where micro-budgeteers can sound as good
or better than the big boys at little or no cost. All it takes
is some listening time.

We left a couple of Overhead items for last. Public-
ity is a category that is often overlooked. While a unit
publicist is an unnecessary and, for those keeping a low
profile, a possibly counterproductive job, someone acting as a still photographer is not. We are not talking about
Polaroids for continuity purposes; besides, at a dollar a
pop, low- and micro-budget shoots should encourage
people to keep continuity the old-fashioned way—with
pencil and paper. As with E&O and a host of other items
that can be taken care of after the picture is finished, all
distributors will want a quantity of color and black-and-

white photographs. Needless to say, these are best taken at the time of shooting. Even ultra-micros can afford a few rolls of slide film. If you really want to save, most cities have labs that process Eastman Color Negative and print slides from them, so you can even load your shortest ends into cassettes and use those for stills. If you cannot afford a still person, at least find someone on the crew who knows how to focus and set an f-stop on a still camera and plan on shooting at least a roll of slides every day.

Did we save the best for last? Maybe. The final account is Miscellaneous and normally includes two pertinent line items. The simplest is an MPAA Certificate and Code Rating. No, the rating isn't free: It costs from one to eight thousand dollars, depending on the budget and who's asking for it (distributors get a price break here). That you can save for later; the real can of worms in Miscellaneous is Legal.

In a real sense, legal transcends the entire budget. It reaches back before production into fund raising and forward into distribution and profit participation. It is, sad to say, lurking behind every sandbag and prop tree, waiting to spring out and make your life miserable. Hopefully, you have limited your personal liability from the start by forming a corporation to own and operate your filmmaking enterprise. The classifieds are full of attorneys who will perform this service for a reasonable fee, or you can buy how-to books. Many people raise money by means of Limited Partnership offerings, which is also fine from a liability standpoint as long as the General Partner is a corporation. Because a corporation is a legal person, its liabilities (debts, legal actions, etc.) do not affect any other persons, at least in theory. California courts have sometimes held the officers and/or directors of a corporation personally liable, particularly if they bent corporate rules of behavior. Nevada or Delaware corporations have stronger protections.

Why be so concerned about liability? Did you skip

some of the previous material, like the stuff on insurance just before this? Unfortunately, there are more than a few producers who abuse the process. A company called American Independent (not the original Nicholson and Arkoff outfit) specialized in $250,000 made-for-video cheapies. When the dunning phone calls from creditors started stacking up like jumbo jets over Kennedy, they just changed the name. Assuming that you are planning on meeting all of your obligations, you still need protection from all those who would overcharge, misappropriate, file nuisance lawsuits, or otherwise try to extort money.

Your finished picture also needs protection. We don't mean just a copyright filing, although that should be done as a matter of course—and costs all of $15 and the price of a video cassette. If you remember what we said about the world's only honest distributor in the last chapter, you won't be surprised to read that there are guys out there who will take a 1/2-inch transfer of your workprint and scratch track with a time code window burned-in, dub it (zooming in to remove the window), equalize the sound, and sell it throughout the Third World from Peru to Singapore. Sound farfetched? It's not. And the only way to prevent this from happening to you is not to hand out copies to anybody you don't know and/or can't trust.

After direct costs come two more items, Contingency and Completion Bond. We talked about the Bond already. It has a lot of implications about the kinds of deals you will be allowed to make, as anything less than standard rate will have to be formalized to be bondable. There is also the bond fee itself. Lower budget means higher risk and higher fee: a net 3% or 3.5% in today's seller's market. (The actual fee is 5% or 6% with a portion, up to half, rebated if the bond is not invaded.)

Completion bonds require contingencies of at least 10%. Sometimes additional amounts for specific risks are also required. Whether or not you have a bond, try to have a contingency. If you don't spend it all, great. On a low-budget, there's a slight chance of that. On a micro-budget? Well, credit cards are the ultimate contingency fund of micro-budgeteers, and anything less than every one of them taken to the max is gravy.

The Scenario

> That's the way you do it.
> Money for nothing,
> And your kicks for free.
> > Mark Knopfler, "Money for Nothing"

All this book really can do is offer constructive suggestions about how to accomplish the goal of making a feature film for 5, 10, or 25,000 dollars per day. Like we've said, the strategies and the stories are true. We or those we know have used them all, not always successfully but always in good faith. This last concept is important, and not just from a legal standpoint. Sometimes side deals are necessary, but if the key to using leverage, to convincing all the cast and crew (which can be a substantial number of people) to come aboard at a low rate is through favored nations, then favored nations it should remain. Anything else is less than good faith on your part.

What this book is really about then is how to write and execute the Scenario. The Scenario is not the screenplay, but the way the picture comes together. Since the Scenarios that have come together for us have differed broadly in budget—never as low as the price of a used car but certainly less than the aforementioned Mercedes 500 and never close to *T2* but nearly reaching eight figures—not all of our experiences have been applicable to *Hollywood on $5,000, $10,000 or $25,000 a Day*. All that, outside of anecdotes, tips and tricks, makes it impossible to impart in any schematic way the method of Hollywood on low- and micro-budgets. To sum it up, we'll take one last trip down the line, above and below, and suggest how it could happen.

The script comes from a friend. She didn't write it but knew you were looking for something that was good, something that could interest cast and crew *and* could be done for a reasonable price. *Key point*: Getting the word out to people you know in the industry is more effective than ads or agents. (If you don't know any people in the industry, maybe you should go out and meet a few before you get too far ahead of yourself.)

Are you producing and directing this picture yourself? If either of these positions is on your search list, the strategy should be similar. Look for people who have done this before. If they have not produced or directed features at your budget level, then people who have worked in music videos, commercials—even industrials—and who are looking for feature credits may be good candidates. Scenario: The producer comes out of the Corman school, where he has line produced and production managed for Corman wages (i.e., peanuts). He'll work for expenses only (i.e., free) because: (1) it's not a schlock Corman script; (2) you've got enough money to make a decent film out of it; and (3) you will share the "Produced by" credit with him. The director comes out of music videos and also wants a feature credit; not so desperately as to work for free, but well below the DGA concept of low-budget rates.

Key points: The producer has done low-budget work before on pictures with even less money than yours. Like we said earlier, don't hire someone, no matter how cheaply they will work or how impressive their résumé, who has only done *bigger* budget shows; it's much easier to step up, slightly or a lot, than to step down. The producer could have also acquired the needed experience in commercials or industrials, but the director should have some more dramatic credits on his or her résumé. You need someone who has dealt with difficult, actor-type

personalities (musicians qualify in spades in this regard—
if you don't believe this, you haven't worked on music
videos) and extracted good performances. This, not flashy
camera work or editing, is the primary criterion. Like we
said, nothing makes a movie seem lower budget than bad
acting. Directors who have worked in theater are a good
alternative. Writers who have never directed anything
(unless it's you, the person who raised the money) are
not a good idea. Neither are assistant directors, directors
of photography, editors, composers, production designers, etc., etc. This is not to say that it's never happened
or never with good results, but why are you giving any
of these people their break with the money that you've
raised? What's the other viable director alternative? Much
as we hate to say it, yes, an actor, an actor who is willing to bring his or her name to your movie for scale in
exchange for the opportunity to direct also. Because,
assuming that actor's name is worth something (if not, see
"why are you . . ." above), he or she is giving you something of real value for that directing shot. In addition,
while not all actors can necessarily be good directors,
actors do know about performance, and we already put
that at the head of the criteria list.

In this Scenario, you've already got a director with
a solid reputation out of music videos. When you send
the script, which is also solid, out through Breakdown
Services, you get some agency interest, but they aren't
sending you any premium names. What you have is a
wish list. You pick one and you make the call. It's time
to sell that agent on your project and what it can do for
the client. First feature for a TV actor? First starring role
for a supporting player? First time as the hero or villain
or doing comedy or drama? You fill in the blank that
seems most convincing. If *your* performance is good
enough, then you will win a prize. All this assumes a SAG
show, in which case scale all around with points and deferments should be your opening offer. Keep remember-

ing "favored nations'; even if you are non-SAG and using unknowns, be equitable in your deals. *Key point*: You don't have money, but as with writer, director, and producer, there are other opportunities that may influence prospective cast members.

If you haven't hired a producer or production manager, then below-the-line will be more directly your concern. Whether you're executive producer or director, if you got the funding, you should still be in a final approval position on all the deals. The Scenario here: Your director has worked with talented photographers and designers in music video and will call in some favors. Caution: If the favor is too great (i.e., the pay cut is too substantial), these talented friends of the director may evaporate faster than dew in Death Valley. Caution Number Two: Even if these department heads will come aboard for much less than their rate, can and/or have they ever worked on the kind of material, budget, and schedule that you can afford? What about their people? Are they all fast friends of the director, too, or will they be looking for their rate. Cheap and slow can be a lot worse than mid-priced and fast in the long run. On the micro-budget, it's time to get some old Corman crew lists (hopefully, you should, at least, be able to offer better working conditions) and post notices at the film schools. *Key point*: They may be less flashy, but conscientious people who know how to stretch a buck are usually your best bet.

What's the rest of the Scenario? As each crew member signs up, they give you the name of others who would be amenable to the arrangement, whether it be lower-than-normal or even partial or full deferments. Crews give out references not just to help you, but to earn brownie points from the reference recipients on future projects. The director of photography has a wild Arri II-C that he throws in as part of the package. The designer just finished a network Movie-Of-The-Week and brings along a lot of discarded set pieces. The propman has a warehouse of material that he makes available for a fraction of normal. The costumer has her own sewing machine, iron, and Polaroid camera, and she shops at Ross Dress for Less. The craft service guy has his own pickup truck and all the paraphernalia. These are the kinds of turns of fortune that mean you may have some of your contingency left, if you could afford a contingency to begin with. Now if Agfa will give you their ultra-secret, triple-dip discount and Fotokem will give you a five-figure credit line with 120 days to pay, you may just have a shot at getting to answer print.

How does the successful Scenario end? With a finished movie, a bidding war, and a two-picture, first-look deal at a major studio. After all, this is Hollywood, the dream factory. Fantasies aside, the winning Scenario is enough sales to give the money back to who ever put it up, give video copies to all the reel builders, and maybe even pay a smidge of deferments. It may not sound like much, but in this day and age, it's the kind of modest success that will let you go again. That, after all, is what it's all about.

APPENDIX 1
BOOKS
(Some Handy, Some Not)

> But if you follow the fashions of the day, you
> will be pallid in hue, have narrow shoulders,
> a narrow chest, a long tongue, small hips and
> a big thing; you will know how to spin forth
> long-winded arguments . . .
>
> Aristophanes, *The Clouds*

What you'll find here is a helpful little (well, maybe not
so little) list of books about filmmaking. Some deal with
the technical side (e.g., What is the aspect ratio of 16mm?)
or budgeting (How much should I offer my grip?) or
packaging your film (How do I sell it to an unsuspecting distributor?) or simply facts about production (What
the hell is a "call sheet"?).

We have surveyed these books and offered you
some—what we hope are helpful—comments on them
so that you won't have to spend your hard-earned dimes
on books you don't need or want (except ours, of course).

As an added note, you may not be able to find some
of these books for sale even if you wanted to buy them.
So save your money and visit a library like the Academy
of Motion Picture Arts and Sciences Library in snooty
Beverly Hills. There's no charge, but you have to read the
books there. If you're not near BH, then raid your local
library. Particularly good are college libraries and bookstores, which try to fill the demands of film classes and
tend to stock at least some of these titles. Good luck.

Before You Shoot: A Guide to Low Budget Film Production.
Helen Garvy.
Shire Press (Santa Cruz, CA), 1985.

Would you pay $10 for a book with a hand-drawn cartoon on the front and pages that look like they were typed and xeroxed? Then when you look closer, you find that the book is filled with even more amateurish cartoons (no Matt Groening here). To what purpose? Maybe to the purpose of filling up the pages so that the publisher can charge more money for the book?

Not to be entirely negative, there is basic information in this book, in a very rudimentary form—and it's not all wrong. The author has done some micro-budget producing, but she doesn't use many real-life examples; are we missing something here? She does have some sample forms, like everyone else, but doesn't bother to fill them in. It's always nice to see how the numbers balance and what manipulations are possible, especially when we're talking micro-budget. There may be a certain appropriateness to producing a book about micro-budget filmmaking on a micro-budget, even to having a character that looks vaguely like Fred Flintstone holding a gun to his head on the cover (talk about your positive attitudes); but books and movies are not analogous. If they were anyone with a word processor and a desktop publisher could crank out a finished feature from the comfort of their own home.

It seems like this book was thrown together without a lot of thought (certainly not like ours).

The Beginning Filmmakers's Guide to Directing.
Renee Harmon.
Walker and Co. (New York), 1993.

The title of this book is somewhat deceptive. It deals with more than directing. It discusses budgeting, screenwriting, camera work, equipment, etc. Get a new title!

The book could also use a few more illustrations. There are the standard forms everyone is now reproducing (for budgets and general production), but let's see some photos. Illustrations help relieve the boredom. And let us tell you, we can get pretty bored reading 185 pages of pure text. This ain't college, you know.

Breaking Through, Selling Out, Dropping Dead.
William S. Mayer.
Limelight Editions (New York), 1971 & 1989.

Everyone who was serious about making films in the '70s (and wasn't that everyone) had this book on his/her shelf. It was a counter-cultural manifesto that each of us memorized. What was so appealing about this book to young filmmakers? There were two things. First, it preached "revolution," actually using that forbidden word in its text. Mayer asked his young readers to take the reins of moviemaking out of the hands of old businessmen and put their own ideas into action.

Secondly, Mayer told you just how to get control of those reins. His advice was practical and included "raising money," "unions," "film schools," "screenplays," "editing," "rehearsing," even "stealing," a section that discussed how your ideas are stolen by the big guys.

Cinematography.
Kris Malkiewicz.
Simon & Schuster (New York), 1973 & 1989.

If you borrow it from a friend, give it to your cinematographer. This book set the standard for books on cinematography. It was at one time used in film classes nationwide because it is so easy to understand, yet thorough.

It is heavily illustrated with photos of lighting equipment, tripods, cameras, filters, sound equipment, editing equipment (that full-page shot of a Nagra is so lifelike). Yes, even though it's only supposed to be about cinematography, the author couldn't resist wandering off topic into the fields of editing, sound recording, and optical printing.

Although this book was originally published in 1973, a revised second edition was published in 1989.

Creative Film-Making.
Kirk Smallman.
Collier-Macmillan (New York), 1969.

The '70s were sure a fertile time for books on filmmaking. We thought everybody was out at the local disco. Smallman's tome is one of those classics of the period. It was used in film schools and was on the shelves of struggling filmmakers everywhere. Its cover is right out of the Beatles *Yellow Submarine* period, and it boasts that you can make a film for only $198, not $199, not $197, but exactly $198. Nowadays, you certainly cannot buy a used car for that amount.

It is also another book that you will have a tough time locating. And when you do, you'll find much of the technical info is out of date. In addition, the publisher is rather brazen in his attempt to make the book longer and, therefore, charge more money for it. Many of the pages are only half-full (or is that half-empty?). Maybe the concept is that the reader will have some place to make notes, but ultimately we have the last laugh: We can't pay anything for the book anymore. It's out of print. Try a library.

Dealmaking in the Film and Television Industry.
Mark Litwak.
Silman-James Press (Los Angeles), 1994.

The only thing wrong with this book is the title. "Dealmaking" implies tips on how to negotiate. The bulk of this book is made up of examples of contracts for writers, directors, actors, et al. While you could scrounge up samples of most of these, isn't it worth a double-sawbuck to have a handy compendium of all of them? What would be really handy is the same forms on magnetic media ready to upload into the old word-processor.

The author of this book is an attorney, and they've known since long before the light bulb went on over Mr. Xerox's head that boilerplate is the name of the game. Being an attorney, he also, after all the usual disclaimers, cuts through the legalese in which most of these documents are mired to explain the key points. Although some of the "you have rights" rhetoric may sometimes sound like an ambulance chaser's infomercial, the tips like how to take a meeting and protect yourself without pulling copyright notices and non-circumvention agreements out of your briefcase are quite useful. There is a passing nod to low-budget filmmakers, templates where the "Very Big Productions" become "Very Independent"; but, in fact, deals are deals. After noting that, from screenwriters to composers, people will work for free, Litwak clearly recognizes that only the numbers need to change. But for good measure, he throws in a sample of a non-SAG actor deal. For those too pressed for time to savor the details (or who might be used to dealing with attorneys on a $200-an-hour basis), there are a lot of sidebars on everything from "Defamation" to an "Actor Career Checklist" (!?). In the text and the glossary, Litwak takes the mystery out of a lot of those buzzwords from "development" to "distribution," buzzwords that sharks like to use as bait for the unwary. In all, a book worth having.

Elements of Film.
Lee R. Bobker.
Harcourt, Brace Jovanovich (New York), 1979.

This is one of those film-as-art books, but a very successful one that has gone into several editions. The author teaches at NYU and is a documentary filmmaker (okay, so he has credentials).

This is the kind of book you pick up if you want to start thinking about making your film "good." And you should be thinking about that all the time. It talks about montage and photographic imagery. It illustrates different lighting styles with some nifty color photos from films such as *Chinatown* and *The Godfather.* You should definitely hope that your cinematographer and your editor give you results that look as good as these examples.

And this book isn't just theory. There are practical suggestions, like how to use sound effects creatively, that any low-budget filmmaker could take into account. Although he refers constantly to A-budget filmmakers like Coppola and Polanski, the principles are the same. If you're bogged down in the mechanics of finance and production, take a break. Here's something that'll raise your spirits.

Feature Film Making At Used Car Prices.
Rick Schmidt.
Penguin (New York), 1988.

Yes, Rick Schmidt is serious, and if you can't figure it out from his title, the subtitle of his book is "How to Write, Produce, Direct, Film, Edit, and Promote a Feature-length Film for less than $10,000." Is this guy for real? At first taste, Schmidt comes off a bit too much the faux naif, but he has made four features within these parameters. What he doesn't tell you is that the way you accomplish all the items in his subtitles is by doing them all yourself. Yes, Schmidt writes, produces, directs, photographs, and edits. He does hire a sound man and a camera assistant while filming, so one presumes that, as the actors take care of their own wardrobe and make-up, props appear as needed on locations, which, according to Schmidt's anecdotes he finds by driving around until smitten and then hopping out to do a soft-shoe for the owner.

As with most micro-budget (or in Schmidt's case, hyper-micro-budget) filmmakers, he is heavily into cajoling, to wit: "I encountered a desk clerk who would absolutely not let us shoot a scene in the driveway of his motel, where I had spent $100 putting the production up for the night. (A whole $100! And no red-carpet treatment from the clerk after Schmidt coughed up a yard for the Presidential Suite?) I begged, I offered money (we can't resist these parenthetical jibes. How much do you think he offered: six bits?), I explained that our movie was ultra-low-budget. Nothing seemed to change his mind. Finally, I told him that making films was, for me, the same as working on his car might be for him. It was my hobby, my love. And here I finally hit the right button. He said he worked on his car and understood, and told me to go ahead and shoot my scene." My hobby, my love? While several of Schmidt's former collaborators have actually gone on to dip their toes into the mainstream, Schmidt had made all of four ultra-low, hyper-micro features in twenty years. Apparently the *El Mariachi* experience has escaped Schmidt.

And don't imagine that he is just putting in time at McDonald's (he was apparently a fry cook at one time, but he doesn't say where), saving his nickels and dimes for years until he can go again. Schmidt says it better than we can: "To make films, I've used money I've earned, sold family antiques, received grants, borrowed money from relatives and friends, charged many thousands at the lab. I've even gone a year without paying rent (thanks to my generous landlord). If you believe that nothing can stop you from making your film, not even money will hold you back." We bit our tongue a lot as we typed that quote. We can only say again, Is this guy for real? We checked the dedication, which is to his six kids (apparently films are not Schmidt's entire life) and not, as it should be, to his generous landlord. Obviously, Schmidt has never tripped over a three-day notice in his unshaken belief than not even money can hold you back.

Still, there is an admirable pluck to Schmidt's escapades. This is a man who makes features on a thread, not a shoestring, who prefers the "communal" experience of using non-actors and a few deferred crew, to whom he diligently assigns points and pays out from his meager film-festival prize monies. This guy is sincere and he does love film, and we have to admire that; and if this is the kind of non-mainstream, art-film experience to which you aspire, it's not too late to take our book back and trade it in for Schmidt's. If you can find his book, that is. The ultimate irony is that Schmidt's homespun effort, wherein he even has diagrams on how to build you own editing bench in your abode in the space reserved for the washer/dryer, has gone into six printings with a major trade publisher, but it's almost impossible to find. No kidding, the only place in Los Angeles that had it in stock was Samuel French.

Feature Films on a Low Budget.
John Randall.
Focal Press (Boston), 1991.

This is a slim, discursive volume that offers a mixed bag of information. The author, John Randall, apparently has a production company in Mexico and has produced and directed some films there. The sample in this book is a Mexican quickie entitled *Deadly Reef* that Randall claims cost around $350K. If the stills of Randall and cast and crew at work are any indication, the people who put up the money did not get full value for their pesos. Randall also reproduces a poster from the film, which he calls the "Spanish language version." *Deadly Reef* is not in any English language video guides that we checked, so if there is an American version, it's news to us.

Maybe Randall's been down Mexico way too long, but his English prose has definitely acquired the flavor typical of a non-native speaker. It's all pretty rudimentary stuff with lots of generalities and a few odd tips. Apparently, a lot of *Deadly Reef* takes place on a cabin cruiser, hence our favorite tip: When you want to shoot reverses, just turn the boat around. Like most of the offerings of the Focal Press, this one is really overpriced; but if you feel the need to pay good money for pointers like this, don't let us dissuade you.

Film and Video Budgets.
Michael Wiese.
Michael Wiese Prods. (Los Angeles), 1990.

Michael Wiese is nothing if not thorough. This book shows you every budget imaginable in detail: student films, student videos, short films (non-student, we guess), film documentaries, video documentaries, music videos in video, music videos on film, low-budget features, concept spots (?), commercial spots, video-magazine segments, video concerts (one hour only, please).

But you have to admire the guy, really. With his Apple II computer using Peachtree's Magic Wand/Peach Text Word processing program and Visicorp's "Visicalc" spreadsheet program (are there actually people out there still using Apple II computers?), he wrote and published quite a precious book here. These 343 pages are chock full of budget information and suggestions on how to save money. In fact, pages 277 through 287 are riddled with bullets identifying money-saving tactics.

Michael Wiese has built a little publishing empire with self-help books like this one. Look at any bookstore with a film section and you'll find his tomes lining the shelves. Keep up the good work, Mike. You strike us as maybe a little uptight and you're probably a neat freak; but we think this wholehearted endorsement (and the ones coming up) of your product rates putting us on your comp list for future releases.

Film and Video Marketing.
Michael Wiese.
Michael Wiese Prods. (Los Angeles), 1989.

Another entry from the Wiese publishing empire. This

one concentrates on marketing, as the title so clearly indicates. Like most of his self-published tomes, Wiese scours the field looking for details that might have escaped other authors on the same subject. Is this one-upmanship?

This time he divides his book into film and video sections. On the film side, he zeroes in on independent films. He tells you to know your product: What genre is it? What audience is it aimed at? This he considers primary in determining how to market a film or video.

He also thinks that ad art is mighty important and illustrates his book with what he considers good poster and cassette-box art. And as he points out, many cassettes of the low-budget ilk are rented on the basis of their covers, especially when there are no recognizable stars. His major case study for his film section is *Dirty Dancing*, barely a low-budget film but what the hey.

His video section is divided in a manner similar to his film section. We especially like the acronym he coins here—POP. (Did he think it up? Well, even if he didn't, let's credit him with it.) POP is the "Power of Packaging." As mentioned above, many a mediocre film (including some of our own) have been sold purely on the basis of the cassette-box art. In fact, some films are repackaged under different titles, given new box art, and released to live yet another life on video.

Film Directing Cinematic Motion.
Steven D. Katz.
Michael Wiese Prods. (Los Angeles), 1992.

This is a companion piece to Katz's *Film Directing Shot by Shot.* If you add this book and its companion together, you have almost 600 pages on the subject of directing alone. Admittedly this book has some interviews with such name people as director-writer John Sayles and cameraman Allen Daviau, but, still, isn't there such a thing as overkill?

We must say that the type is much larger and easier to read than in Katz's other book and the illustrations are sometimes full-page, but between the two books you've got quite an arduous film course. Does the Wiese Publishing Empire make such demands on all their authors?

Not coincidentally, words like "workshop" and "textbook" keep popping up on the covers of both books. Must you wear your heart on your sleeve? Don't worry, film schools will pick these up.

Film Directing Shot by Shot.
Steven D. Katz.
Michael Wiese Prods. (Los Angeles), 1991.

This book is banking on becoming a textbook. It looks, feels, and smells like one. In fact, it looks a little like a physics text we had in high school, filled with charts featuring arrows going every which way and points labeled "A," "B," and "C." It's all a little overwhelming. But as with most of the books published by the Wiese Empire, it is complete and to the point. There are pages and pages of sample storyboards, several ways to block a particular scene, whether it be a three-character scene or an action chase, numerous methods for laying out a tracking shot.

However, as with most textbooks, this to me does require some study. We spent at least twenty minutes trying to figure out those flow charts. But I suppose it's worth it. Just wish we had to study less.

The Film Director's Team.
Alain Silver and Elizabeth Ward.
Silman-James Press (Los Angeles), 1993.

The second edition of this book sure has a blinding cover. Grey, green, blue, and white patches are a little too much for our retinas. But we guess it grabs your attention. Silver and Ward's tome describes the work of the assistant director and the production manager, key people in any well-run production. This book details their jobs, giving an excess of examples of how they're done. There are reproductions of call sheets, budget breakdowns, production boards for both TV and low-budget films. There are camera reports, SAG agreements, releases, and the de rigueur glossary of film terms.

Their sample film is *The Creature Wasn't Nice,* a.k.a. (the second edition informs us) *Spaceship.* Has anyone anywhere seen this movie? Leslie Nielsen before *Naked Gun* and Cindy Williams after *Laverne* sounds like a real gobbler. Judging from one of the sample call sheets, it even had Paul Brinegar. Wasn't this guy "Wishbone," the cook on *Rawhide?* Where did they unearth him? We also think that the chapter called "The Working Professional: A Panel Discussion" is padding, pure and simple. Who wants to hear a bunch of ADs and UPMs tell war stories and crack bad jokes? If you do a next edition, guys, lose it. Overall, it's not a bad book; but your production manager and ADs are hopefully already aware of its contents.

Film Finance and Distribution: A Dictionary of Terms.
John W. Cones.
Silman-James Press (Los Angeles), 1992.

We hate books that alphabetize several words as if they were one word. It goes against everything those nuns taught us in grade school. Children, children, "B-movie" comes before "Backend" not after "Blurbs." Don't this guy Cones got no education? Seriously, folks, we had to go fourteen pages out of our way because we alphabetize the old-fashioned way, the way every library in the world does it.

Well, venting out of the way, this is quite a "little" book. It brags that it has more than 500 pages of finance and distribution terms, and this is no idle brag. According to the author's two-page biography, this guy is a lawyer, lobbyist, and dealmaker and should know from whence he speaks.

Each term is given ample definition and treated with great seriousness (unlike other glossaries, which are far too flippant). One could pick up more jargon from this book than from a convention of entertainment lawyers, and we hope that the thought of such a gathering doesn't make you shudder too profoundly. If you're producing a low-budget film, and we assume you're at least thinking about it (or why else would you be holding this book?), then you are going to encounter a lot of these terms. So get a jump on it. Read the whole thing and dazzle your potential investors with terms like "pro and con analysis" and "borrowing base formula."

Film Lighting.
Kris Malkiewicz.
Simon & Schuster (New York), 1986.

This is another book from which your cinematographer might have cribbed, along with Malkiewicz's other classic, *Cinematography*. The book is divided into sections like "Lighting Equipment," "Image Manipulation," "Lighting on Location," and each of these sections has noteworthy cinematographers and gaffers such as John Alonzo, Vilmos Zsigmond, Richmond Aguilar, and James Wong Howe waxing profound on the subject.

It's basically a cinema-as-art book, but you've got to get the crew to think that way some of the time or you're going to end up with another unreleasable slasher film no one wants to see. The book is fully illustrated with photos that show lots of different kinds of lighting set-ups and the moods they create. What's also good is that Kris isn't too highfalutin' to print a picture of a nooklite or a skylite for those of us who haven't seen one.

Film Producing: Low-Budget Films That Sell.
Renee Harmon.
Samuel French Trade (Hollywood), 1988.

Renee Harmon's book is another excellent aid. It is

thorough. In fact, its table of contents alone is three pages long. Harmon leaves nothing to the imagination. Under "Advertising," she includes one sheets, slicks, lobby displays, radio spots, TV spots, and trailers. She even has a discussion of "Why Capable Actors Face Difficulties in Front of the Camera," not a subject usually treated in a book on film producing. Hey, every little bit of advice helps.

We also find it edifying that she concentrates on your film's prospectus. This is often overlooked in other books on the subject, and shouldn't be because this document can be crucial in attracting investors with either money or in-kind contributions. It must look professional and use some degree of legal language. She also lays out the standard parts of a prospectus: synopsis, project status, development plan, and budget. You might want to use this book to raise the money, which our book tells you how to spend.

Her discussion of distribution is pretty enlightening too. She has a real knack for getting at the core of the issue and drawing out the facts you need to know.

Film Scheduling.
Ralph Singleton.
Lone Eagle (Los Angeles), 1984.

Subtitled "Or How Long Will It Take to Shoot Your Movie," this is the "classic" and most widely distributed how-to on scheduling, using Coppola's *The Conversation* as its example. Breaking down a script and turning the result into strips on a production board is a task best learned by doing, and Singleton's coded step-by-step is a reasonable guide; but, despite the color end papers, it's really no better than the forms and samples in other books such as *Film Director's Team*. Moreover, in order to use this book, you have to buy companion work-books, so don't be deceived and think that it's complete in one volume. (Singleton and Lone Eagle have been promising a companion volume on Budgeting for years, since before their *Budgeting Workbook* came out in 1985; and it may finally appear in 1994, completed by Robert Koster.)

One wonders about such glaring errors as "Breakdown Page Number: This number should correspond to the scene number unless the script you are breaking down has been numbered previously and there are scenes which have been ADDED [bold and caps his] (usually noted by a letter following a scene number, e.g., 24A) . . ." What? Obviously, Singleton had not encountered scripts where master scenes, such as two ends of a telephone conversation, are intercut; or where writers-who-want-to-be-directors put in close-up, inserts, etc. No matter how many "shot numbers" there are, all of a master scene can and should be put on one breakdown page. Maybe somebody forgot to stop and think. Anyway, many if not most scripts are not shooting scripts and don't have any numbers, and it might be good to devote more than a couple of sentences to lining and numbering a script.

Filmmakers' Guide to Super-8.
Eds: *Super-8 Filmmaker* magazine editors.
Sheptow Publishing (San Francisco), 1980.

"You don't need a cigar to be a producer or a beret to be a director. You don't even need sunglasses to be a star. In the world of Super-8 filmmaking, you can be all these things—all by yourself . . ." So begins the naive introduction to this now-dated book on Super-8. Yes, the world of Super-8 has shrunk considerably since those halcyon days of 1980. Equipment is disappearing, labs are fewer. And the promise of Super-8 becoming a viable format for cassette or cable TV has not panned out.

However, if you are forced into that format, this book along with Lenny Lipton's classic, would be indispensable—although we can't imagine why you're shooting in Super-8. Didn't you read the beginning of this book? Aren't you listening to us?

The Filmmakers' Handbook.
Edward Pincus and Steven Ascher.
New American Library (New York), 1984.

This book is an updated version of a now-out-of-print standard, *Guide to Filmmaking* by Pincus sans Ascher. It is a technical survey of filmmaking. It covers in sufficient detail the areas of editing, film stocks, light meters, cameras, sound, lighting, editing (sound and picture), lenses, and laboratories.

Good indexes are really a help in a technical book, and this is a good one. If you don't know what a diopter is, it leads you right to the page. If you're having trouble remembering if the lower the f-stop, the more light the lens lets in or vice versa, this book answers your question in a flip of the page.

The book also shows you some nice depth-of-field charts (we always forget to memorize those) and a whole section on cement splicing (yipes!).

Filmmaking: A Practical Guide.
Carl Linder.
Prentice-Hall (New Jersey), 1976.

Don't you just hate it when authors put photos from their own obscure films in books and then talk about them as if they were the movies of John Ford? We do. Carl Linder sticks in photos from his film *The Devil Is Dead* (are we supposed to know this movie?) and identifies them as "The Gluttony Scene" and "The Castration Scene." Then he proceeds to discuss them right next to such classics as *The 400 Blows* and *Breathless.* Doesn't this guy have any shame?

This book is oriented toward those interested in experimental filmmaking. Linder has long sections on what he calls "The Expressionistic Film" and on "Working with Pure Structure" (as opposed to working with "Impure Structure"). This all sounds like academic flapdoodle to us. But if you're interested in such stuff, maybe you should pick up the book. Seek and you shall find it. We know not where.

Financing Your Film.
Trisha Curran.
Praeger (New York), 1986.

This book tries to lead you through the treacherous waters of film financing. It's very user-friendly, featuring lots of checklists at the end of chapters to allow you to review the material you've just read. (Boy, you can tell this woman is a teacher!)

She gives sound advice about appealing to the glamour factor of the movies when selling your project to non-industry investors. She also, with her business background, supplies a lot of legal advice and info that is valuable to the novice.

The most valuable part of the book to us is the detailing of a low-budget film (*Lianna*) from beginning to end, including limited-partnership forms, financial statements, and profit sharing agreements. She also gives a sample budget, which is always welcome for those not familiar with that crucial component of filmmaking.

Grammar of the Film Language.
Daniel Arijon.
Silman-James (Los Angeles), 1991.

This is the paperback edition of a book that was originally published in hardcover in 1976. According to the intro, it's a self-proclaimed classic, having been translated into numerous languages—including "Serbo-Croate."

The first thing that impressed us was the drawings in this book. There must be 400 of them, showing every possible angle, camera movement, match cut, composition imaginable. It's all very film-school. In fact, this looks like another book jockeying for position as a film-school text. There's big money in that, you know. We do have a question about those drawings. Even though the first thing we noticed was that all the women in the drawings have deep cleavage, and are eventually nude, why is everyone, male and female, wearing dark glasses? Maybe their future's so bright they have to wear shades.

We do think, however, that the author has gone a bit overboard in trying to explain subjects such as camera movement, tracking, zooming, match cutting, character placement, etc. Some of his explanations are a bit dense, while his drawings are so crosshatched with arrows and other details that they resemble the schematics for a jet engine. A little more simplicity, please. Our brain is already overloaded.

The Hollywood Guide to Film Budgeting and Script Breakdown for Low Budget Features.
Danford Chamness.
Stanley J. Brooks (Los Angeles), 1988 (5th Edition).

Could there be a more overblown title or a more useless book? What this man does not know about scheduling and budgeting could fill a multi-volume set. Of course, he makes up for it by using a TV-pilot script that he wrote himself and reproducing it in its entirety as a sample. Great literature, it ain't. What did you think, Dan, some producer was going to read your "sample" and option it? Some producer probably did; but who cares? Don't buy this book; if you believe in bad vibes, don't even touch it, and if someone gives you a copy, burn it.

The Hollywood Job Hunter's Survival Guide.
Hugh Taylor.
Lone Eagle Publishing (Los Angeles), 1993.

From the photo of the author on the back, this looks like some Yuppie's "Survival Guide." And it is. Any book that lists restaurants to eat at and includes the Bistro and Chasen's, or tells you where to rent or buy your cellular phone, hey, that's Yuppie.

To be honest, though, this guy is pretty thorough. He

writes the book for somebody who's interested in getting an entry-level job as an assistant of some sort in a big studio, a talent agency, or some humongous entertainment corp. He doesn't assume the potential applicant knows anything (even where to eat, we guess). He tells you how to answer the phone and take messages and file. Oh well, all of us need help at different levels.

Our favorite section is "Arranging a Trip for Your Boss." No stone is left unturned—every detail, from his limousine to not ignoring the "needs and desires of the boss's spouse, or whatever . . ." What "needs" might those be? And who is "whatever"?

This book is of little value for the world of low-budget filmmaking, unless you want to give it to your secretary, if you can afford one.

How To Shoot a Movie and Video Story.
Arthur L. Gaskill and David A. Englander.
Morgan and Morgan (New York), 1985.

This book is in its fourth edition. It must be good, right? Written way back in 1947 (was there TV back then?), it's been updated a little each edition.

The book is very nuts-and-bolts. It explains close-ups, zoom lenses, match cutting, cutaways, etc. It's real Basic Film Production 101. But if you don't have that info, then you should take a look at it. Of course, the question is, If you don't know what a "close-up" is, why are you making a feature film? Ours is not to reason why.

The book of course covers the other basics, too. What is a "pan"? What is a "dolly"? How do you frame? (Boy, we're getting bored writing about this. Imagine if you have to read it.) But if you're that far behind, then grab the book and brush up your film terms.

Independent Feature Film Production.
Gregory Goodell.
St. Martin's Press (New York), 1982.

This tome has some mighty impressive endorsers on

the back: one-time Academy President Fay Kanin, directors John Carpenter and Ridley Scott, and editor Verna Fields. They seem to think that this is the best thing to come down the pike since sliced bread. And it's not bad. (The book, we mean, not sliced bread. We like muffins ourselves.)

Goodell is very conscientious about what he covers. He starts with financing, moves into pre-production, which includes the budget and screenplay. In production, he discusses organization, call sheets, production boards, etc. After a great deal of detail on post-production, he tries to give you an idea of the markets and how to approach them.

It's a good solid survey of the independent feature-film terrain from A-Z.

The Independent Film and Videomakers Guide.
Michael Wiese.
Michael Wiese Prods. (Los Angeles), 1990.

This book is another of the offerings of the Wiese Publishing Empire, on whose comp list we should, by now, be permanently placed. As he says himself in a bit of naked self-promotion, this book is a "classic best-seller." It's easy to see why.

Wiese takes the reader through financing, partnership agreements, income projections, investor presentations, and distribution, including cable and home-video markets. He spends a lot of time carefully explaining what's involved in these areas, how you can package, finance, and sell your product.

The price of the book is even reasonable: $18.95 for a book of almost 400 pages. Also he fills it with examples of agreements and forms, always valuable to the struggling low-budget filmmaker.

Independent Filmmaking.

Lenny Lipton.

Straight Arrow Books (San Francisco), 1973.

Yes, another nostalgia book from the '70s. Aren't you glad "retro" is in? You'll have a tough time finding this baby, though, and some of the info on film stocks, equipment, etc., will be definitely old-hat. But if you can make compensations for that, the book is still a solid technical survey of what you should know about independent filmmaking.

Formats covered are from Super-8, Double-8, and Single-8 ("What the hell are those," you ask? If you have to ask, you're too young to know) through 16mm and Super-16mm. Cameras are shown as well as dissected in more technical detail than anyone other than a cameraman (excuse us, camera person) might want to know. The same treatment is given sound and editing. How do you mix soundtracks? What is the difference between an optical and magnetic soundtrack? How do you sync up dailies? All those and many other burning questions are answered for you and you alone.

And to top it all off, there's a glowing intro from experimental superstar Stan Brakhage. He strokes Lenny's ego plenty. But it's all deserved. If only this book had been updated, we could have given it a higher rating on the Gaines-Rhodes scale.

LA 411.

Deborah Goldblatt, ed.

LA 411 Publishing Co. (Los Angeles), 1990.

This is a book you really need to cough up the cash for (and it's a significant cough). But the book has everything you wanted to know about union rules, stages, talent agencies, production companies, equipment-rental houses, prop houses, wardrobe rentals, post-production facilities, support services and were afraid to ask. It even has a section called, coyly enough, "everything else."

This book gets bigger each time they publish it. Yes, they do update it frequently. The 1993 edition was at least two inches thick. It has a lot of ads, admittedly, but those can be helpful sometimes. They're usually for equipment-rental outfits who are advertising their wares.

The best thing about this volume is that every entry has a corresponding telephone number and address. Need a cheap sound stage? Turn to page 62 and you have such a range that your head will begin to spin. And not just the big stages, but smaller, cheaper ones, the kind you probably need. Need a dog and his trainer, it's there. Need a snake and her trainer, it's there. You won't be disappointed. (Where have I heard that before?)

But honestly, folks, what other book is going to give you the phone numbers of masseurs and masseuses who come on to the set and sushi restaurants that deliver (or is that masseuses who deliver?).

Lipton on Filmmaking.
Lenny Lipton.
Simon and Schuster (New York), 1979.

One of the lesser books by Super-8 guru Lipton. It is a collection of articles by the master on varying subjects, mostly technical—his field of expertise.

As an example of how dated a book can become in little more than a decade, check out the article on "Weddings in Super-8." Lipton spends five pages discussing the best way to shoot a wedding. He even includes some nifty photos. Great. But when is the last time you saw a wedding photographed in Super-8? 1980? Now that weddings and almost all the home market have become video's sole domain, Lenny should do some field work at Disneyland some weekend and count the Super-8 cameras. There might be one or two toted by some tourists from Tierra del Fuego. It's time for *Lipton on Filmmaking* to go out of print.

Low Budget Features.
William O. Brown.
Brown Publishing (Los Angeles), 1975.

Back in the 1970s before the flood of books about filmmakers and filmmaking, this was the bible, or at least one of the bibles, of low-budget filmmakers. Every film school had a copy in its library. It told you everything you needed to know to make a film. And it did it in a concise, to-the-point way. It was filled with illustrations showing rental forms, budget breakdowns, call sheets, etc., before every book and its brother (or sister) had them. And it even gave you some sample rental costs and places to get equipment.

It began with organizing and financing the film and led you through formats, script breakdowns, production boards, shooting schedules, and budgets. It told you honestly what people you needed on a low-budget crew and who you didn't. And Brown didn't mince any words about his recommendations. Under "Assistant Hairdresser" he wrote "Forget about it." Our kind of guy.

We know that this all sounds like a eulogy for a dead friend. In a way it is. This book was our first practical guide to the world of low-budget; but we do have to warn the buyer. It is terribly out of date in its information about prices, film stocks; even locations of business are now inaccurate. So even though we recommend the basic approach, the details are now fuzzy. So maybe you should go with a more recent book. Too bad, old pal.

Making Movies: The Inside Guide to Independent Movie Production.
John Russo.
Dell (New York), 1989.

How can you hate a book that advertises on its cover, "The Film School in a Book"? What cojones! Hey, now don't you feel foolish having spent thousands on an education at UCLA or, worse yet, USC, when you could've dropped $9.95 ($12.95 in Canada) and gotten the same thing?

There are some valuable sections of this book, despite its arrogance. Independent filmmakers, or former independent filmmakers, such as Tobe Hooper, Lizzie Borden, Oliver Stone, and George Romero, do tell some long-winded but informative tales about their careers. You can always learn from those more successful than yourself, as long as they don't hit you in the face with it. And maybe someday some young-pup writer will be interviewing you about your wild and windy career in the movies. "Tell us, sir, how did you do it?" "Well, son . . ."

Mascelli's Cine Workbook.
John V. Mascelli.
Cine/Grafic Publications (Hollywood), 1973.

Are we "lost in the '70s" yet? Bell-bottom pants, here we come. This is another "text" of the period. *Mascelli's Cine Workbook* was a great Christmas gift for a struggling filmmaker. It had everything in it. It wasn't just a book. It had focal length charts, color charts, viewing filters, exposure calculators, even a grease pencil. And the back cover was a slate! All for $15, which, come to think of it, wasn't such a bargain twenty years ago.

The book is unfortunately out of print, so it hasn't been updated for decades; but it was nifty while it lasted. We could spend hours just staring through that color viewing filter. No need for hallucinogens when this book was around.

Motion Picture Marketing and Distribution.
Fred Goldberg.
Focal Press (Boston), 1991.

Focal Press has an extensive series of how-to books on the film and television industries, a lot of them by ex-black-listee director Edward Dmytryk, which are discussed below. They are all overpriced.

This is a must-read for those of you unsure of what to do about distribution and marketing, or even for those who are sure but want to learn a little bit more. The author has forty-five years of experience toiling in the fields of marketing and distribution in the employ of heavyweight studios like UA, Columbia, and Orion. He has no mean résumé and is not shy about flaunting it.

Goldberg takes you through the maze-like world of marketing and distribution. He tells you what kinds of deals you can expect for video-cassette rights, pay-TV sales, and theatrical distribution. He shows you how to design trailers, radio spots, press kits (audio and print). The illustrations are nifty, too. The book has examples of posters, storyboards for trailers, licensing agreements, distribution agreements, to mention a few.

The statistics in the book are mind-boggling, a lot of them from *Variety*, one of the industry's two trade organs. He quotes them ad infinitum and, if you can absorb it all, you end up with a pretty good sense of what the market out there is like and how you get at it.

The Movie Business.
Jason E. Squire (Ed.).
Simon and Schuster (New York), 1983 & 1982.

This book boasts the likes of Mel Brooks, Robert Evans, William Goldman, and Sydney Pollack as contributors (no lightweights here). It is divided into eleven parts, including "Property," "The Money," "The Management," "The Deal," "The Selling," and each of these sections has some words for the wise from luminaries in the field (no, not Klieg lights).

The quality of the essays vary. Some are to the point, like AD Murphy's on "Distribution and Exhibition." Of course, Murphy has been studying these things for years and is a perennial source of statistics for the trade newspapers. If you're after more gossip and less facts, then there's always the master raconteur Mel Brooks, whose entry is called "My Movies: The Collision of Art and Money."

Movie Making: A Guide to Film Production.
Sumner Glimcher and Warren Johnson.
Washington Square Press (New York), 1975.

It's another blast from the past, like William O. Brown's book, which will be hard to find outside of libraries. Also, some of the material inside about film stocks and equipment is woefully dated.

It is, nonetheless, a landmark book, one of the first to say on its back cover in bold letters "You Can Make a Movie." It empowered young filmmakers who never had a chance in the studios, or who never even wanted a chance in the studios, to go out and do it their way. And around the country youngsters with bright faces and little dough asked, "How? Show me how?" This the authors did, from planning the project to showing the film.

Even though it is pocketbook size, it is literally stuffed with illustrations and text that answer dumb questions, not just "How do you use a light meter?" but "What is a light meter?" If you can dig up a copy, it'll probably be a collector's item. Guard it carefully.

New Poverty Row.
Fred Olen Ray
McFarland and Co. (Jefferson, NC), 1991.

Not only do we love this title, but who else could have done the subject justice like a seasoned practitioner? None other than Fred Olen Ray. Now that Tim Burton has immortalized Ed Wood, could guys like Fred and Jim Wynorski, guys who can direct such classics as *Texas Chainsaw Hookers* or *Sorority House Massacre II*, have a real shot at being taken seriously? We don't think so, but it would appear that Fred himself, who illustrates his little book with scores of garish poster reproductions in living black-and-white, does. McFarland specializes in selling obscure books for lots of bucks, but this one is at least worth a look. A lot of the filmmakers and companies that Fred chronicles are as defunct as their predecessors in the original Poverty Row, but the concept lives on. A lot of the observations culled from interviews and personal experience confirm that veteran low-budgeteers are very aware of what can be accomplished for no money and plan accordingly.

The filmographies provide more detail than just about anyone, including the people who worked on them, would ever want about these minimalist wonders. This only proves that Fred can't pad a book as well as he can a movie. Fred, it's a visual medium. You should have used more stills of Brinke Stevens drooling or Delia Shepard topless, but not in one of those ridiculous clinches with Jay Richardson. By the way, why do you keep using this guy, Fred? Is he giving you a kickback? You'd be better off mixing and matching the Bottoms Brothers. Then maybe you could get invited to visit Joe Bob like Wynorski did.

Off Hollywood.
David Rosen with Peter Hamilton.
Grove Weidenfeld (New York), 1987.

Sponsored by the Sundance Institute and the Independent Feature Project, both firm supporters of struggling independent moviemakers, this book traces the history of thirteen independent films from financing through distribution. The films include *El Norte, Eating Raoul, Hollywood Shuffle, Return of the Secaucus 7,* and *Stand and Deliver.*

You can learn a lot from reading these stories of the trials and tribulations of these films because they all ended up victorious in the end. They passed the test. You should know their titles. If you don't, look in our video section and head for your local Blockbuster.

None of the stories can, however, top that of *El Norte's,* which included attacks by bandits, negatives held for ransom, live rats biting actors, and storms in the Mayan highlands. Read it, you'll love it. Then see the movie, if you haven't already.

There are also some nice appendices showing the cash flow of theatrical distribution monies and ancillary market returns. There's a particularly nifty graph (we like those) that shows you what you, the filmmaker, might expect to make on a distribution deal. Don't be depressed. Just grin and bear it.

On Screen Directing.
Edward Dmytryk.
Focal Press (Boston), 1984.

We have never seen so many pictures of an author in his own book (hey, by the way, where are our pictures?). Every other photo is of "the director, Dmytryk" with this actor, "the director, Dmytryk" planning this shot. All right, enough of the family photo album. Some modesty, please.

Edward Dmytryk is an okay director who did a series of really interesting lower-budget films in the '40s—*Crossfire, Murder, My Sweet,* and *Cornered*—was blacklisted for a time, then named names in order to work again and never made a good film after that. (Is this like karma or something?)

"The director" regales us with story after story about his career while supposedly telling us about casting, set design, lenses, editing, dubbing, etc. He does have some worthwhile tips, though. His section on how to get along with cast and crew members, including rooting out potential "malingerers" as he calls them (is this a hangover from McCarthy?), can be of value when you're shooting fast and dirty and have to depend heavily on your crew for support.

A Primer for Filmmaking.
Win Sharples, Jr. and Kenneth Roberts.
Macmillan (New York), 1971.

As a survey of the technical end of filmmaking in

16mm and 35mm, it is so dated that it would be hard to recommend the book. It is also difficult to find, like most books of that decade that haven't been reprinted.

It does, however, have a good discussion of "The Aesthetics of Film Editing." It talks about montage, Eisenstein, temporal and spatial continuity, stage lines, etc., things that are timeless. It also illustrates the discussion with examples from movies. Each page has at least two or three illustrations, which help you understand the concepts.

Producing, Financing, and Distributing Film.
Paul Baumgarten, Donald C. Farber, and Mark Fleischer. Limelight (New York), 1992.

This is a revised edition of the classic book on producing, financing, and distributing film (that's the title, isn't it?). It's slick, it's well-written, and it's worth the price of admission.

The book surveys how you acquire a literary property, including optioning, granting rights, etc. Under "The Screenplay Agreement," the authors tell you about items like WGA minimums and standard payment for scripts. Under "Production-Financing and Distribution Agreement," the writers eat up a good amount of pages dealing with insurance for the cast and completion bonds for the film as well as liability insurance for the period of shooting—items you don't normally like to think about but should, depending on the size of your budget.

Agreements of various kinds are a major concern to these guys: artists' agreements, directors' agreements, producers' agreements. The writers obviously have a background in law because they're really anxious that you don't get sued. And all this legal advice is only $17.95 as opposed to $200 per hour in some fancy lawyer's office. Can't lose on this book. An ounce of prevention is worth a pound of cure. The cliches are flying today.

Reel Exposure.
Steven Jay Rubin.
Broadway Press (Shelter Island), 1991.

Here's a neat little book (actually, it's quite a large book) that specializes. It takes on the subject of publicizing and promoting your film. It tells a novice how to put together press kits, production junkets, test screenings, and advertising campaigns.

To say that the author of this 337-page epic is compulsive is an understatement. Our favorite example is under "screenings" when he tells you to establish a "rapport" with your projectionist. This guy has obviously not had many dealings with projectionists. They are a solitary breed. The last projectionist with whom we tried to "establish a rapport" nearly shoved a used carbon rod down our editorial throats. (What's a carbon rod? If you know, that will tell you how long it's been since we tried to establish rapport with a projectionist.) But seriously, this author's treatable neurosis is your gain. Just page through the table of contents. You won't be disappointed. But watch out for those projectionists.

Roll 'em! Action! How to Produce a Motion Picture on a Shoestring Budget.
Harry M. Joyner, Jr.
McFarland and Co. (Jefferson, NC),1994

This book was originally self-published under the title *Making a Video Feature on a Bare Bones Budget* (the new edition doesn't mention this, but our usual assiduous research turned up that little-known fact in the publisher's catalog). When you read the preface about the author taking a cigar box with "2,000 pennies" and buying his first 8mm camera, hopefully you won't be so far from the store that you can't walk back to the counter and demand a refund of your 3,000 pennies plus tax.

Joyner is a self-proclaimed hick from the sticks who must still spend a lot of time in his basement designing arcane alternatives to professional equipment, preferably fashioned from native spruce. This is not to say that the man isn't well meaning, but his style makes Rick Schmidt read like Tom Clancy. Here's someone who delights in giving you a tip on how to shoot your beach scenes indoors using sawdust instead of sand because it's lighter and cheaper. Wouldn't it be easier just to go to the beach? Then, of course, there's the page after page of material on glass mattes and hanging miniatures! If the author had more spare time, he could probably progress from fabricating his own lights and dollies out of materials from the local landfill to larger items like cranes and honeywagons. The bottom line in this book is just like everywhere else: You beg, borrow, or build all the equipment and get a bunch of amateurs to work for free. Joyner throws in a lot of technical terms and quasi-jargon without explanation and has some priceless anecdotes about running the same piece of film through the camera twice: "That's right. We shot that roll and, *somehow in the confusion* [italics ours], loaded it up and shot it again." Earlier, Joyner described how a half-dozen strategically placed crew members fired "thirty-six Roman candles" at an actress "protected only by a thin wall of Plexiglas": "They went over the set, under the set, into the set, and into the tile ceiling. It looked like the Fourth of July." Kids, don't try this at home. People actually hire this guy to do work for them?

If anything needs a disclaimer or, at least, an expiration date, it's Joyner's appendix of production forms. These items were stale in the '70s. This book even reproduces a copyright form. Of course, it's the wrong one (TX rather than PA); but these things happen. Hey, don't run that film through the camera again. We've already used it three times!

Scare Tactics.
John Russo.
Dell (New York), 1992.
What a great cover! Color stills of stakes through

hearts, bleeding, ulcerous faces, and throats being cut. That should sell a few copies. This is a handbook, if you couldn't guess, for making horror movies of the gore type. The author is an expert at it, having written, produced, or directed over ten low-budget chillers.

If you are making a horror film, this might be a worthwhile investment. Besides Russo's sage advice, you have the wisdom of such goremeisters as Clive Barker, John Landis, Rick Baker, and Joe Dante. The emphasis in the book is always practical. He covers not only the nuts and bolts of scripting, budgeting, and production, but he also talks about how to promote the script at the investment stage and then sell the finished movie later.

Russo also devotes pages to following the paper trail of several of his own films from novel to cassette release, including a vampire epic called *Heartstopper.* Ever heard of it? Neither have we. If you've got the money and can put up with the cover, buy it.

The Super-8 Book.
Lenny Lipton.
Straight Arrow Books (San Francisco), 1975.

This the definitive, and we do mean "definitive," book on Super-8 filmmaking. Every Super-8 film class in the country back in the '70s and '80s had this as their text. (Well, maybe not every class. We have been known to exaggerate.)

Lipton was Mr. Super-8. If his book couldn't answer the question, then the question must be wrong. He even covered the area of projection in Super-8, something the other books hardly touched.

But what made his book so appealing was his lack of pretentiousness. Look at the quote at the beginning of the book: "And further, by these my son, be admonished: of making many books there is no end, and much study is the weariness of the flesh." (From the Bible no less.) This is true hippie, flower-power thinking. Enough of these endless books. Go out in nature and, with camera in hand, make your own history.

The usefulness of Lenny's book has pretty much petered out. It's a rare find, like much of Super-8 equipment. But if you do find a copy, hold on to it dearly, for us. And if for some reason you are forced to shoot in Super-8, this is the book for you.

Super-8 Handbook.
George D. Glenn and Charles B. Scholz.
Howard W. Samms and Co. (Indianapolis), 1980.

So much of this book is already out of date in only fourteen years. Super-8 is heading for the toilet (didn't we say this already? Maybe it's time to flush), so recommending any book on this format is counterproductive. If we have to give our imprimatur, it would be on Lenny Lipton's books. They're the most comprehensive and reliable, although their info is outdated, too (tempus fugit).

If you must shoot in Super-8 (why must you?), find Lipton's books. Search libraries, film schools, used bookstores. If you can't find them, then get whatever you can, including this book or any other that looks half-decent.

The Work of the Motion Picture Cameraman.
Freddie Young and Paul Petzold.
Hastings House (New York), 1972.

Now here's a beautiful-looking book and by (at least, half-by) one of the great cinematographers of all time—Freddie Young (*Lust for Life*, *Lawrence of Arabia*, *Lord Jim*, etc.). It's hard-bound and priced accordingly, but the photos alone are worth the price of admission. They are high quality, almost giving you a sense of what the original picture might look like. Almost, but not quite. But it'll send you running to your local video store to see a few of Freddie's films (Young, of course, not Krueger).

The book also contains 236 small-print pages of information covering items from generators to types of incandescent lighting, from light meters to camera movement, from wide screen to shooting snow. It's all here. Again, as with all older books, some of the technical info may be dated, but there is enough theory and general advice to overcome technical deficiencies.

Working Cinema: Learning from the Masters.
Roy Paul Madsen.
Wadsworth Publishing (Belmont, CA), 1990.

Here's a cinema-as-art book in which you could drown your troubles for a few hours to escape the rigors of low-budget filmmaking. Maybe you'll even get an idea or two from it. After spending days trying to figure out your potential markets, your licensing agreements, your bottom line for props, it'll be a healthy experience. Think "art."

We actually mean it, honest to God, sort of. Learn from the masters. After all, you don't want your film looking like a TV show. See what Vilmos Zsigmond has to say about lenses, composition, lighting and "relationships" (does he mean, like lovers?). See what Dean Tavoularis has to say about "the designer's role" and "relationships." (There's that word again. Is this a pop-psych self-help book or what?) See what Hanna-Barbera has to say about the art of animation. "Art and animation?" Hanna-Barbera? Fred Flintstone? On second thought, you might want to skip that part.

Oldies but Goodies

Writing how-to books on filmmaking goes back a long way. These are rare titles, but they can be found in libraries and might help put things in perspective, as only books written long before you were even born can sometimes do.

Film Production.
Adrian Brunel.
Newnes (London), 1936.

How can you fault a book that has a section on "Hairdressing for the Screen" by Biddy Chrystal? Brunel started out making satirical shorts and seems to have kept his tongue in cheek through most of this discursive little volume. There are chapters on "Cruising" (on a ship, not down a boulevard) and the various materials from which one can fabricate "Reflectors." For blocked writers, there's even a chapter on devising character names and a long list in the Appendices. Well, all these little details add up, or, as Biddy observes, "There is an art to 'undressing' as well as dressing hair; it can be made to look quite attractive, even though wet or entirely disordered . . . so hairdressing, in its way, is very essential to the making of a picture."

Working for the Films.
Oswell Blakeston, ed.
The Focal Press (London), 1947.

How can you beat this: Freddie Young on cinematography and David Lean on directing twenty-five years before *Lawrence of Arabia*? This is also an all-British cast, and they take themselves very seriously, but there are some great two-color charts suitable for framing, especially the one comparing U.S. and British production using stylized celluloid strips with an eagle and lion perched on the ends. This book also has a list of union working conditions and the "approximate minimum weekly wage: for all movie jobs." Who knows but that showing a gaffer that his or her British equivalent made 7 pounds 4 shillings and 11 pence a week in 1947 might put things in perspective for that person before making a deal. The book ranges from Lean's shot-by-shot analysis of Laurel and Hardy comedies to Alberto Cavalcanti's self-described cocktail-party definition of producing: "I don't mean to imply that there is anything fundamentally wrong with practical training. Nevertheless, it entails a great waste of time and energy." Now there's food for thought. The bluntest opinion comes from art director David Rawlings: "The producer must make money or the industry will kill itself, as such. Films must be made more cheaply—not only half as cheaply, but at a fraction of their present cost." A fraction of 7 pounds a week for the Number One Juicer? Roger Corman ought to frame that quote.

Your Career in Motion Pictures.
Charles Reed Jones.
Sheridan (New York), 1949.

Who bought these books? A friend of ours owns a copy autographed to Dana Andrews (one of the contributors) by the author. This book has quite a contents page from Gregg Toland on feature photography and Edith Head on costume design to Veronica Lake on "Getting Started as an Extra" (we bet that there are some untold stories there). While most of these are anecdotal essays about how the authors broke in, filled with all the necessary examples of hard work and high resolve, some of them are still remarkably pertinent. Veronica Lake's chapter is, in fact, full of statistics and lists of requirements that, if anything, seem designed to discourage Midwesterners from taking a bus to Hollywood to find extra work. Read this after watching *Sullivan's Travels*. The highlight of the book for us is art director Leo Kuter. He remarks briefly but lucidly on the evolution of the industry as a whole and even includes a contemporary top sheet, with typical accounts expressed as a percentage of the whole, that is quite illuminating.

APPENDIX 2
VIDEOS

Video, et gaudeo.
William Shakespeare, *Love's Labour Lost*

Here's a list of films that we think you should take a look at. They range from super low-budget to medium budget, but they were all made on what today's Hollywood would call a "shoestring." The reason you should take a look at these is to get some concepts, if you're lacking those, and to see how a good filmmaker can really utilize his limited resources. We've also tried to pick films that are not only good but represent a particular type of film, like detective films of the 1940s or blaxploitation films of the '70s. All of these films are available on video, although a few of them you might have to hunt for. It's worth the trouble. Video, et gaudeo. Watch and enjoy.

After Dark, My Sweet (1990).
Director: James Foley.
This adaptation of hard-boiled novelist Jim Thompson is classic limited-budget filmmaking. It has three main characters, and almost all its action takes place in the desert in a few locations. It's hard-hitting and filled with twists.

After Hours (1985).
Director: Martin Scorsese.
Several of Scorsese's films are must-sees for anyone trying to be creative and resourceful at the same time.

This is one of them. This story of a frustrated Yuppie who finds himself caught up in a nightmare of kinky sex, murder, and debauchery uses the NY locations Scorsese loves with intensity and humor.

Alice in the City (1974).
Director: Wim Wenders.

Those Europeans are the masters of shooting on a shoestring. Give them a camera, a few actors, and a ticket to ride and they'll return with a film. *Alice in the City* is just that kind of film. It's the story an alienated journalist who finds a nine-year-old girl who's abandoned by her mother. Together they travel Europe in search of her home. During the course of the film, they both learn a lot about commitment and caring. Well, it's not quite as saccharine as it sounds.

The Ballad of Gregorio Cortez (1982).
Director: Robert M. Young.

We talk about this one in the book. It's one of the few features shot on Super-16, and it looks great. The story is a true one based on the manhunt for—and wrongful conviction of—a Mexican by U.S. lawmen. Edward James Olmos as Cortez gives one of the earliest of his trademark brooding performances.

Bedlam (1946).
Director: Mark Robson.

This is one in a series of films produced and written by Val Lewton at RKO in the 1940s. It is a brilliant period piece and harrowing expose of 18th Century insane asylums. His budgets were minuscule and his shooting schedules laughable, but you believe every minute of this film—even Boris Karloff in a periwig.

Belizaire the Cajun (1986).
Director: Glen Pitre.

This is a period piece that evokes the Louisiana of the

1800s with a minimum of sets and stars. It also uses more handheld camera than Zefferelli in *Romeo and Juliet.* The music is great and Armand Assante as Belizaire has the accent down pat. It's a lot of fun.

Billy Jack (1971).
Director: Tom Laughlin.

This film is not really very good unless you like pseudo-liberal pontificating, but it's worth noting because it made a fortune as one of the largest-grossing films of 1971. Considering it was shot for next to nothing is amazing enough, but Laughlin is a Hollywood legend for buying the film back from Warner Bros. and four-walling it himself so that he, not the distributors, made the fortune. Too bad he squandered it on sequels and bizarre remakes. We're told that this is a guy who had a Moviola on the set so his Western based on Hideo Gosha's samurai classic *Goyokin* could be a shot-for-shot remake. He's had *Billy Jack Goes to Washington* on the shelf for over fifteen years because the character dies in that picture, and he couldn't seem to finish *The Return of Billy Jack.* Amazing is an understatement. In the original, look for lots of locations, few sets, no stars, but a strong story, which goes over the top but with a bang. Laughlin never made another film of its equal, and by the time he actually ran for President of the United States in 1992, most moviegoing voters had forgotten *Billy Jack.*

Black Sunday (1960).
Director: Mario Bava.

Mario Bava is the king of the Italian Gothic horror film. He shoots in abandoned castles to save on construction, uses shadowy photography and fog to hide cheap sets, and zooms rather than tracks in order to speed up the shooting. And the films look like a million (at least lire if not dollars).

Blood Simple (1984).
Director: Joel Coen (and, uncredited, Ethan Coen).

This film was a cause célèbre of the critics. They ate it up. The Coen Brothers were the new Hitchcock by committee. Although the film is not to all tastes (including ours: too much Hitchcock, too little Coen), it is slickly made and at times suspenseful, all on a limited budget.

Boxcar Bertha (1972).
Director: Martin Scorsese.

You can always learn from Scorsese. This time, working for Roger Corman, he took the true story of a free-thinking radical woman (played by Barbara Hershey in her free-thinking, pre-lip-job days), who rode trains and had sex at her pleasure, and came up with an action-packed, funny, and thoughtful cheapie. Just like the boss ordered. Don't miss the precursor of Willem Dafoe's crucifixion in *The Last Temptation of Christ* when Scorsese nails David Carradine to the side of a boxcar.

Car Wash (1976).
Director: Michael Schultz.

This is a perfect example of a film that confines most of its action to one location and still works. Using an existing car wash, it tells the story of the lives of the people working there. It's also one of the few films in Hollywood that focuses on everyday people, of different ethnic backgrounds, who are dealing with everyday problems.

Carnival of Souls (1962).
Director: Herk Harvey.

Is that a great name or what? Herk Harvey! This is a little gem just recently discovered. It was made on a shoestring and distributed on the drive-in circuit, where most horror films met their fate. Today, people see it for what it is: an eerie, imaginative movie with great visual flair about a woman who dies in a car crash but doesn't know it. You don't believe us? Go watch it.

Cat People (1942).

Director: Jacques Tourneur.

Another Val Lewton film that manages to create a mood of suspense and an atmosphere of fear within strict budgetary limitations. This one centers on the psychological dysfunctions of a young woman who changes into a panther under stress. (We've met a few women like that.) Compare this to the big-budget Paul Schrader remake and then tell us Simone Simon isn't cattier than Nastassja ("new, more pretentious spelling") Kinski.

Coffy (1973).

Director: Jack Hill.

The first in a series of blaxploitation films starring the Amazonian Pam Grier (actually, the 6'2" Tamara Dobson was a lot taller as Cleopatra Jones; but Grier was built like a linebacker). It's the best of the group, delivering sensual sex scenes and taut action, with Grier usually doing the delivering. And thrown in for good measure is a social message. What else can you ask for?

The Conversation (1974).

Director: Francis Ford Coppola.

We know Coppola is no longer known for making tight little films on limited budgets, but he was once. *The Conversation* is a brilliant piece of filmmaking shot on location in San Francisco. It's a suspense film with an alienated Gene Hackman as a detective obsessed with his own privacy whose world is exploded by the twists and turns of a new case.

Criss Cross (1948).

Director: Robert Siodmak.

It's a gritty caper film where no one can be trusted, not even (or especially) your lover. There's a lot of stylish L.A. locations, including old Angel's Flight. Like most movies of the film noir type, it was shot with great panache but on a short schedule and a tight budget. It's a classic.

D.O.A. (1949).
Director: Rudolph Mate.

Great taut thriller of a guy dying from radiation poisoning who has to race the clock in order to find his killers. When he does, he dies. Again, there are a lot of locations and no big stars, but it's one of the best films of the period. It's also p.d. (public domain), so if you want it playing on the television on the background of a scene, you wouldn't be the first, but it's no clearance problem.

Delusion (1991).
Director: Carl Colpaert.

A really good example that ended on the cutting room floor when we locked our main text. This picture is a pastiche of film noir elements that was planned for a few hundred thousand and could have been pulled off at that budget. It's got several classic twists and a small cast in a remote setting (Death Valley). Extra money didn't really help make it better, but it turned out pretty well.

Dementia 13 (1963).
Director: Francis Ford Coppola.

This super-low-budget film produced for Roger Corman is discussed in the text. Don't look for too many precursors of *Bram Stoker's Dracula* here, but "the unbearable atmosphere of mounting menace" got *Dementia 13* fourteenth place on frightmeister Stephen King's scariest-movies-of-all-time list.

Detour (1945).
Director: Edgar G. Ulmer.

Yes, another basically silly classic from the '40s. This is the one where Tom Neal (of *Hollywood Babylon* ménage à trois fame) inadvertently strangles a woman in the room next door when she gets tangled up in a telephone cord. Whoa. This film has such a rep that it's come to epitomize cheapjack existentialism. It's even been remade recently, practically shot for shot. If that isn't a homage, we don't know what the word means.

Diary of a Hitman (1992).
Director: Roy London.

Look this one up in the main text. Limited sets and actors and a lot of messages on answering machines get the plot across cheaply.

Easy Rider (1969).
Director: Dennis Hopper.

This is the film that convinced the studios that there was a youth market who wanted to see films about themselves. It was so financially successful that every studio went out and recruited filmmakers right out of the film schools. Although the film is terribly dated, too, in which the '60s come off a drugged-up, early heavy-metal days, it was a breakthrough movie.

Eating Raoul (1982).
Director: Paul Bartel.

This film is beyond "camp." Bartel limits his locations, uses minor actors, and mixes sex with cannibalism. How you can not love a movie in which the Real Don Steele and a score of assorted sycophants are electrocuted in a Bel-Air pool? It all works and is hilarious to boot. But why do they keep making Broadway musicals out of low-budget, man-eating, black comedies?

Five Corners (1988).
Director: Tony Bill.

This is one of those slice-of-life movies. It gives you a neighborhood, several characters, and their dramatic problems. There's a lot of location shooting to save dough and some great performances from Jodie Foster and John Turturro. It's not action-packed, but you'll never see a more harrowing scene than when Turturro tosses his mother out the window.

Five Easy Pieces (1970).
Director: Bob Rafelson.

Another breakthrough film. Like *Easy Rider*, it's rebellious and alienated and a little insipid, with lead Jack Nicholson rejecting all the values of Middle America (now there's a reach). Jack's bantering with a snotty waitress is a transcendent movie moment. How many viewers always wanted to do that but were too wimpy to try?

The 400 Blows (1959).
Director: Francois Truffaut.

ʾhis film is the beginning of the French New Wave. These young guys took to the streets with their cameras. In films like Godard's *Breathless* and this one by Truffaut, they redefined low-budget art. The films were dirt cheap, often using handheld cameras and grainy black-and-white stock. But the stories were great and the characters memorable, so the world plunked down its change to see what these boys were up to next.

Frankenhooker (1990).
Director: Frank Henenlotter.

Yes, *Frankenhooker*. These guys crossed the Frankenstein story with the world's oldest profession and got a funny, often bloody, movie about a guy who reconstructs his girl with hooker parts. Unfortunately, she has a tendency to walk the streets at night and give johns more than they reckoned for. It's become a midnight-movie staple, and it's perfect for that campy audience.

Girlfriends (1978).
Director: Claudia Weill.

This is a streetwise film about a young woman's

struggle with careers and men. It has real, everyday emotions and a nifty performance by Melanie Mayron in the lead, before she lost all that weight and got a nose job.

Gun Crazy (1950).
Director: Joseph H. Lewis.

This movie shows you what you can really do on a low budget. It has energy, wit, and a patina of psychological depth. It even has a great bank robbery, done in one take, and shot from the back seat of a car. The psychosexual fire between the two young lovers is hot, even by today's standards. They love their guns as much as they do each other.

Guncrazy (1993).
Director: Tamra Davis.

Not a remake of the 1950 film (can't you see that it's spelled differently?), this movie has its own sexual energy. Drew Barrymore's performance as part-nymphet, part-coldblooded killer is a wonder to behold. Director Davis broke out of the music-video world with this feature and uses her resources (less than $1 million) to the max, giving the film a gritty, naturalistic feel.

Halloween (1978).
Director: John Carpenter.

This film is often held responsible (or at least shares the credit with the original *Friday the 13th* made two years later) for initiating the slasher-film fad. Shot on the cheap (reputedly under $200,000), it was one of the top-grossing films of the year. And it's a lot better than most of its imitators.

Hester Street (1975).
Director: Joan Micklin Silver.

This is a period piece that was shot low-budget. That's quite a challenge. It tells the story of a Jewish immigrant woman who comes to New York and tries to hold on to her past. It has a great sense of detail in costumes and locations and, consequently, looks a lot more expensive than it was. That's always a good sign.

The Hills Have Eyes (1977).
Director: Wes Craven.

Wes Craven has done more to change the face of the low-budget horror film than any other director in the last two decades. His *Nightmare on Elm Street* spawned a whole series teen-nightmare films as well as the ubiquitous Freddy Krueger and his many imitators. Craven's films are intelligent and literate and are always about something bigger than just "slice and dice." *The Hills Have Eyes* is one of his early efforts. It's all shot in the desert with almost no sets, but it's a tense exercise in horror with a Middle American family pursued by its opposite, a deranged family of Neanderthal throwbacks. In the end, can you tell the difference between the two? That's Craven's point.

Hollywood Shuffle (1987).
Director: Robert Townsend.

Townsend creates a gentle satire of the situation of African Americans struggling to find a job in Hollywood. Shot on weekends with borrowed equipment and leftover film for a little over $100,000, Townsend and many of his collaborators have gone on to bigger things and are all part of a renaissance of black filmmakers over the last decade led by Spike Lee. Most began shooting on shoestrings, and now have the studios begging to tie their shoestrings.

The Horseplayer (1991).
Director: Kurt Voss.

One of those "weird folks come out of the woodwork in L.A." movies made for a few hundred thou. Brad Dourif actually portrays a guy wearing a ski mask and parka because his job is to sit in a cooler and to restock the shelves as consumers remove bottles and cans from them. A truly strange occupation, but somebody has to do it. Occasionally he goes to the track (hence the title). His life is cold contentment until even weirder folks move in next door. The late Vic Tayback is great as the Middle Eastern liquor-store owner.

The House of Usher (1960).
Director: Roger Corman.

You can always learn from Corman. Here he takes three actors, one large mansion set (which he uses over and over again in other films), and a great spooky Poe story and mixes it together. Voila! Instant classic and a big moneymaker, too.

I Bury the Living (1958).
Director: Albert Band.

You might call this a pre-Full Moon, pre-Empire cheapie from the *eminence grise* of the Band family. With craggy thespians like Richard Boone and Theo Bikel to chew the scenery, how could one go wrong? The premise is simple: Boone's character inherits a cemetery and discovers that, when he puts a black pin instead of a white one into the newly purchased plot, the person dies. Well, of course, he can't resist trying it again. Could you? A minimalist triumph.

Invaders from Mars (1953).
Director: William Cameron Menzies.

Menzies is the genius designer behind such epics as *Gone with the Wind*. In this film, he took all that talent and reworked it in a lower-budget frame. The sets still look wonderful, all stylized to look like the nightmare of a small boy who thinks that aliens have taken over his world.

Killer's Kiss (1955).

Director: Stanley Kubrick.

Yes, even mega-budget, *2001* Kubrick started out making quick-and-dirty films like this one. Kubrick did everything on this one, except sweep up at night: director, writer, editor, photographer. It's a tough, romantic film about a boxer in love, a plot that got revamped into *Stranger's Kiss.*

Kiss Me Deadly (1955).

Director: Robert Aldrich.

A couple of hundred thousand went a lot farther back in 1955 when director Aldrich and writer Bezzerides junked Mickey Spillane's "steamy" (yes, steamy—more has changed since 1955 than the price of milk) novel and set a wise-cracking, lip-curling Ralph Meeker chasing Pandora's box all over L.A. from Bunker Hill to the Hollywood Athletic Club until a mushroom cloud over Malibu fries what's left of the cast. If that's not enough "pretty pow" for you (see the movie, you'll understand), you're too jaded.

Lianna (1983).

Director: John Sayles.

John Sayles is a director who has specialized in the low-budget film. He earns his money writing scripts for bigger-budgeted schlock and then re-funnels the proceeds into his own, very personal movies. His films deal with topics Hollywood usually doesn't touch: lesbianism (*Lianna*), union organizing (*Matewan*), or interracial science-fiction (*The Brother from Another Planet*). We recommend renting all of the above. You'll learn more about filmmaking than you can handle.

The Little Shop of Horrors (1960).

Director: Roger Corman.

If there is a more-celebrated feature film shot faster

or cheaper than this one, we'd like to know its name. Who else could have brought this epic forth but Roger Corman?

El Mariachi (1993).
Director: Robert Rodriguez.

Look in the text for this one. We christened it a micro-budget classic there.

Mean Streets (1973).
Director: Martin Scorsese.

Mean Streets has all the feel of a home movie about your neighborhood. A lot of the film is handheld, the photography is grainy, and the cutting jumpy. The film centers on three friends of very different personalities and how they react to the environment of "Little Italy," NY.

Medium Cool (1969).
Director: Haskell Wexler.

This film was half-shot as a documentary on the disturbances during the 1968 Democratic Convention in Chicago. Wexler took the documentary footage and added a storyline, did some more shooting with actors, and ended up with a classic of low-budget filmmaking. All this was before Wexler became a prestigious, mainstream cinematographer.

Ms. 45 (1981).
Director: Abel Ferrara.

Ferrara has specialized in the lower-budget thriller, including *Fear City* and *King of New York*, but this early effort is his best. Zoe Tamerlis plays a mute seamstress who is raped and transformed into a sexy avenging angel. It's shot on location in New York and has the sights, sounds, and smells of the city down pat. The last scene features a novel mix of underscore and image, so that saxophone notes on the soundtrack seem to be played by a trumpet on screen.

Murder My Sweet (1944).
Director: Edward Dmytryk.

This is the celebrated adaptation of Raymond Chandler's hard-boiled novel *Farewell, My Lovely*. Director-later-turned-teacher-and-author Dmytryk captures the toughness of the main character and the tone of romantic despair that Chandler cherished, all on a B-budget.

My Dinner with Andre (1981).
Director: Louis Malle.

Now here's an idea for a cheap movie: one location, a restaurant; two actors; and 110 minutes of conversation. Well, that's *My Dinner with Andre*. And it was a success of sorts, at least in the art-theater circuit. But, seriously, the conversation is scintillating!

The Narrow Margin (1952).
Director: Richard Fleischer.

This tense film is mostly set on a speeding train as a tough cop tries to bring a gangster's widow to trial. Because the action is confined to one set (the train), the budget of the film can remain low. But this doesn't harm the tension of the movie at all. It increases it. You know, speeding trains, sex, murder—they all go together.

Native Son (1986).
Director: Jerrold Freedman.

This is an adaptation of the novel by Richard Wright. It was done with partial funding from the Corporation for Public Broadcasting but had a theatrical release. It's a stylish period film from a source story that probes the depths of racism in American culture.

Night of the Living Dead (1968).
Director: George Romero.

This is another landmark horror film. Shot in Pittsburgh in black and white with newsreel-style photography, the film is dirt cheap. But it's a killer. The attack of the zombies on the innocent victims barricaded inside is unforgettable. Romero did several sequels to this films with larger budgets, but none had the urgency of this one. Goes to show you that bigger budgets do not a better film make. Haven't we said that before?

Nightforce (1988).
Director: Lawrence D. Foldes.
A classic example of how not to do it—see main text.

El Norte (1983).
Director: Gregory Nava.
We talked about this one earlier. We don't want to repeat ourselves more than we already have.

One False Move (1992).
Director: Carl Franklin.
This is a sleeper of a film that caught the eye of the critics but not the public. Rent it. It fulfills all the requirements of this book. It's relatively low-budget, it's intelligent, it's tense, and it's about something—in this case, love and racism.

Over the Edge (1979).
Director: Jonathan Kaplan.
Here's a film about bored kids in the wastelands of suburbia. They're bored, they're destructive, and they're your kids. Great promo line, huh? (This picture was originally called *Mousepacks*. Get it?) Kaplan makes good use of razed lots of land waiting for a new mall, suburban tract houses, and prison-like schools, all locations in Denver (no sets, please).

Phantasm (1979).
Director: Don Coscarelli.
It's in the text.

A Polish Vampire in Burbank (1985).
Director: Mark Pirro.
In the text.

Polyester (1981).
Director: John Waters.
Waters has been making low-budget "black comedies" since *Mondo Trasho* in 1970. His aim is to outrage and he succeeds. In *Polyester*, he used "scratch-and-sniff" cards so that audiences could enjoy the smell of perfume as well as cringe at transvestite star Divine's flatulence. Unfortunately, or fortunately depending on your particular tastes (or is it smells?), the cards are not available when you rent the video.

The Rain People (1969).
Director: Francis Ford Coppola.
This is, like *Easy Rider*, a road film. The filmmaker picks a road and follows his or her character down it. It's cheap and can be dramatic if the character meets the right people. In this case, the pregnant housewife escaping her humdrum life does.

Return of the Secaucus 7 (1980).
Director: John Sayles.
It's in the text. (We're getting really tired of typing that.)

Ride the Whirlwind (1966).
Director: Monte Hellman.
You guessed it: it's in the text. Jack Nicholson as a cowboy killer? Shot back-to-back with *The Shooting* on a Cormanesque budget.

Riot in Cell Block 11 (1954).
Director: Don Siegel.
Once again, limiting yourself to basically one loca-

tion gives you a lot of leeway to spend money in other areas. This is a violent, claustrophobic film that captures the animalistic quality of prison life.

sex, lies, and videotape (1989).
Director: Stephen Soderbergh.

The title says it all. It doesn't deliver all that it promises (Laura San Giacomo does romp around in simulated sex scenes) and would not rate high on the Joe Bob meter, but it turned a lot of critical heads and metamorphosed into Kafka.

Shock Corridor (1963).
Director: Samuel Fuller.

Fuller is the hard-boiled director-writer of such thoughtful action pics as *The Naked Kiss* and *Underworld USA* and a fave rave of the French critics (maybe that's why he moved to Paris). This film is typical Fuller fodder, a bizarre tale of a journalist who has himself committed to a mental institution in order to investigate a murder and then finds he can't get out. Again, it's mainly one location. Sam Fuller loves to recount how he shot the final scene in which the hero imagines that it rains inside the asylum. They waited until the last day of shooting then used a fire hose on the sound stage at Raleigh Studios and walked away. Not recommended if you ever want to shoot at that studio again.

The Shooting (1966).
Director: Monte Hellman.

Yes, it is in the text. See also *Ride the Whirlwind.*

Smithereens (1982).
Director: Susan Seidelman.

This is a sassy film from the director of *Desperately Seeking Susan.* It's shot in the lofts, clubs, and streets of New York, mainly at night, for less than $100,000.

The Stone Boy (1984).

Director: Christopher Cain.

The is a rural film with a strong performance from Robert Duvall. It has the look and feel of a Faulkner story, all on a minimal budget. The work of cinematographer Juan Ruiz Anchia is extraordinary.

Stranger's Kiss (1983).

Director: Matthew Chapman.

A pickup deal from Orion classics on a real shoestring budget. See text for details.

Stripped to Kill (1987).

Director: Katt Shea Ruben.

This film and its quasi-sequel, *Stripped to Kill II* (what else?), are, despite their titles, effective chillers done for Roger Corman. Most of the action takes place in the strip clubs with a few side locations. Nevertheless, the characters are well-drawn and the acting good, particularly Kay Lenz as the undercover policewoman who gets caught up in her role.

Supervixens (1975).

Director: Russ Meyer.

How can you have a book on low-budget filmmaking and not talk about Russ Meyer. Russ Meyer has created his own little universe of big busts and fast cutting, oblivious to what else is going on in the world. Each film is the same, only the busts and budgets get larger.

Sweet Sweetback's Baadasssss Song (1971).

Director: Melvin Van Peebles.

The studios were so impressed with how much this low-budget film made that they jumped on the black-film bandwagon. Of course, most of what they made was trash, but this film still holds up. It's uncompromising in its indictment of white America and is filled with sex and violence, earning it an X rating. As an interesting foot-note, Van Peebles' son Mario is now at the forefront of the second wave of black filmmaking with films such as *New Jack City*.

The Terror (1963).
Director: Roger Corman.

We're tired of talking about Corman. It's in the text anyway. If you didn't believe Nicholson as a gunslinger, imagine him as a French officer in Napoleon's grande armee, who loses his way and runs into Boris Karloff.

The Texas Chainsaw Massacre (1974).
Director: Tobe Hooper.

In the text.

That Obscure Object of Desire (1977).
Director: Luis Buñuel.

Buñuel is really a case study in how to use your re-sources wisely. He is famous for always coming in on budget and on time, and his budgets were not that large. This film is a perfect example. When his lead actress was unable to continue with shooting, did Buñuel throw up his arms in despair, trash all his footage, and go beg the producers for more money? No, he hired another actress, who did not even resemble the first, and continued shoot-ing. The film he created in the editing room is considered a brilliant depiction of the two sides of a woman's per-sonality, a schizophrenic tour de force. Voila!

You're a Big Boy Now (1966).
Director: Francis Ford Coppola.

This film began as Coppola's thesis film at UCLA and ended up being picked up by a studio. It's a zany com-edy about sex and teenage angst.

GLOSSARY

We really did not want to create yet another useless Glossary of insider terms and stupid buzzwords. Reluctantly, because we didn't pause in our breathless rush to throw out information and because it gives us a chance for a few parting bon mots, we are throwing in the Webril wipe (see below) and doing one. We are, however, only including terms that we actually used in the text. Since we used the term Gaffer instead of Chief Lighting Electrician and never even said Best Boy, you won't find them below. Nor will you find c-stands, flags (French or otherwise), or any size of apple box. You will find a Taco Cart.

Above-the-line. Talent. See "The Line" (under "L" not "T").

AMPTP. The Alliance of Motion Picture and Television Producers, which is the bargaining agent between the major studios and independents and the guilds and unions. This used to be the "Association of," etc. (and is still referred to as the "Association" by some) until Paramount and Universal bolted to make their own deals. They have since returned to the fold under the new banner. Not to be confused with the MPAA, although they are now (or were until the big quake) housed in the same building in the San Fernando Valley. A former location at Beverly and La Cienega, which is not Hollywood but closer, is immortalized as the center of the Studio Zone.

Anamorphic. A curved lens developed for aerial reconnaissance in World War I that 20th Century-Fox turned into CinemaScope in the '50s. This lens bends the image going into the camera, which means that theater projectors must use similar lenses to unbend it while screening—otherwise, even Roseanne Barr would look tall and skinny.

Arm's length. We're not attorneys so we shouldn't mess with this one. Think about it. You can figure it out.

Associate Producer. The movie equivalent of a green-stamp premium.

The "Bad" List. Companies who have invoked the ire of a guild or union by not paying as promised. Most producers who do this regularly just form new companies with a different relative in charge and keep on doing business as usual.

Basic Agreement. The general terms under which members of guilds and unions work. The AMPTP negotiates these on behalf of the producers.

B-Film. A lower grade of film than A.

Below-the-Line. Technical staff and materiel. See "The Line."

Breakdown conditions. To work for less than the minimum rates or allowances called for in the basic union contract.

Corman. A.k.a. Roger Corman, American International whiz kid of the Edgar Allan Poe series and the little shop of two-day wonders; admirer of Bergman and Truffaut; director of the very occasional studio picture such as *St. Valentine's Day Massacre* with Jason Robards as Al Capone (no typecasting there); founder of New World Pictures (sold for a bundle) and Concorde/New Horizons (still operating), not to mention Roger and Julie Music (BMI), the Hammond Lumber school of filmmaking in Venice, California; and anything else that might put a few more coins into his legendarily tight fists. In short, The King.

Day Player. Actor paid by the day. Can also refer to supplemental members of the crew hired on a daily basis.

DGA. Directors Guild of America, which also represents unit production managers and assistant directors, in feature films and television.

Dummies. We prefer throwing jibes at moving targets, so we'll just say that these are either the straw-filled, man-sized rag dolls that *really* look like a human body when thrown from the top of tall buildings *or* a device that plays back an interlocked reel of magnetic film during a sprocket mix.

Edge numbers. A sequence of numbers and letters that appear at every foot of negative film and are used as a guide for matching a "locked" workprint and cutting the negative.

F-stop. Exposure index expressed as the ratio of the diaphragm opening to the lens focal length (now doesn't that sound like a real Glossary entry?).

Favored nations. A phrase lifted from diplomatic parlance to indicate a deal that cannot be bettered. For example, an actor may accept a dressing room on the honeywagon and not insist on a motorhome only on the understanding that he or she has favored-nations status, so that if any actors hired later are given better accommodations, he or she will get that, also. With crew, favored nations implies that nobody will get a better rate for analogous work.

Fill. Any piece of film used as spacer between isolated pieces of music or sound effects. Old release prints are typically used as fill and are much cheaper per foot than mag stock.

Fringes. Things that go around the tops of surreys. Also, one of two types of additional payments that must be factored into labor costs. Government fringes are the employer's share of Social Security, unemployment insurance, and the like, which is calculated as a percentage of all salaries. Union fringes are the employer's contribution to pension, health, and welfare funds, which are calculated as a percentage of union salaries.

Gaffer. The Chief Lighting Technician. Can you believe the IA wants you to put that overblown term (instead of "gaffer") in your end credits now? We prefer Head Juicer (see below).

Grip. Person who works for the Key (see below).

Honeywagon. We're not going to touch this one with a ten-foot pole, and it's a good idea to stay upwind of it, too, as this is the industry term for the truck-and-trailer combo that provides portable dressing rooms for actors and toilets for the crew.

IATSE. The International Alliance of Theatrical Stage Employees—talk about a labor organization that needs a reality check. Do even 10% of the members of the Hollywood locals still qualify for the health plan?

Juicer. An electrician, as in one who provides juice for the lights. Also, a small appliance for turning fruits and vegetables into liquids featured in many infomercials and occasionally seen on health-food-conscious craft service tables.

Kem. Not a typo for Barbie's main squeeze, but a brand name of editorial table on which those cutting film perform their surgery. A typical eight-plate Kem can lock up two reels of picture and two of sound.

Key Grip. The grip (see above) in charge. If you expect us to go on at length about what grips do, from pushing dollies to pulling out wild walls to setting out silks on high rollers to hanging hostess trays on car doors, we'd be here all day and up to our armpits (appropriate metaphorical choice for grips) in jargon, so guess again. You probably want to know so you can explain that T-shirt of yours that says, "Get a Grip on Yourself" to your parents. Why don't you get a special-effects T-shirt instead, the one that says, "The Hell with Dialogue, Let's Blow Something Up."

Limbo. In Christian theology, the place where the unbaptized souls of the Just go to await the Second

Coming. In Movie theology, the place where the prop-less bodies of the actors stand to await the Set Decorator's coming, i.e., a couple of flats or a cyclorama painted some n.d. color with maybe a little smoke around the edges.

The Line. Drawn across the Budget top sheet to divide talent (above) from technical staff and materials (below)

Locked. When the bolt is thrown and the door won't open. Also, in post-production terms when (1) two or more elements of a film are running in synchronization; or (2) when the final cut of a workprint has been made and a locked picture is available for final music and sound work and/or negative cutting.

mm. Acronym for millimeter, one thousandth of a meter, which is 39.37 inches. (In capital letters, an acronym for Marilyn Monroe.) Why, after winning every battle against the unnatural advances of the metric system, are motion-picture film gauges in millimeters? Search us. If you want to start a new trend, 35mm film is 1.377 inches. One-and-three-eighths? Sounds like a socket wrench, but that could work; .629 inches for 16mm or .315 for 8mm might be a little tougher to sell.

MTV. Acronym for "music television," a mystery to all over thirty, which is why they spun off VH-1. A good place to watch directors' reels in the privacy of your own home, although micro-budgeteers might want to concentrate on the "Basement Tapes."

Macs. The big ones are sold by McDonald's and may occasionally be used to feed a crew. The others are Apple computers, less popular than IBM clones for breaking down and budgeting scripts, but still the mainstay in the music part of the film industry.

Midi. An acronym for "musical instrument digital interface" which permits a computer to record input or playback through a synthesizer or other electronic instrument.

Moviola. As with people who refer to any photocopier as the "Xerox machine," Moviola is a brand name that has become generic for the upright, motor-driven editing tools. Like Kem and Steenbeck, Moviola now markets a flatbed editing machine.

N.D. Acronym for "nondescript", i.e., any person, place, or thing which is entirely unremarkable or ordinary-looking.

Off-line. Using an inexpensive video-editing system and dubs of master tapes to make editing decisions before going to on-line. Off-line produces the video equivalent of a workprint, using time codes rather than edge numbers to guide the assembly of an on-line master. It is also possible to transfer film footage to video with the edge number information included and cut a low-budget feature using off-line techniques.

On-line. The final assembly of a video master embodying all effects, titles, etc.

Practical. An interior, such as a restaurant or nightclub (but it can also refer to a living room or a dentist's office), shot on location rather than on a sound stage.

Sachler head. A panning and tilting, fluid mount for cameras that has replaced the O'Connor as the first choice of camera persons and is much smaller and lighter that the Worrell-style gear heads. (This should prove to you that we can write a straight Glossary entry.)

SAG. Acronym for the Screen Actors Guild, mighty representative of all movie thespians and the conferrers of his first presidency upon Ronald Reagan. If that doesn't tell you enough, check with them in Hollywood or at regional offices in New York, Chicago, Dallas, and assorted other cities.

Scale. The mini-mountain you must conquer to hire SAG actors, DGA directors, etc. The minimum compensation permitted under the terms of the Basic Agreement between the guilds and the AMPTP.

Shiny Boards. Silver-metallic reflectors used to bounce sunlight onto people, places, and things.

Shunt time. The few seconds expended when the interlocked picture and sound are reset for another pass during a mix. These few seconds quickly add up to several hours.

Ski pole. An aluminum or fiberglass stick pointed at one end and with handle on the other, used to guide oneself downhill while on skis. Also a favorite horror-movie prop, right after knives and axes.

Sprocket mix. When you throw a bunch of sprockets in a bag and shake well. Also, when all the sound work is done on and/or transferred to 35mm magnetic film for the final mix so that the picture and sound elements are kept in synchronization mechanically by means of the sprockets on the films' edges.

Studio Zone. A.k.a. the Zone. This is not the mind state into which athletes slip. The zone is the thirty-mile circle inside of which guild and union members may be asked to report to location rather than driven to it. This might be significant if you have SAG actors who are not with the program, as most of Orange and Ventura counties are outside the zone.

T2. Acronym for *Terminator 2: Judgment Day*.

T3. Hypothetical acronym for *Terminator 3*: Most Expensive Sequel to a Sequel in Film History.

Taco Cart. A term of unknown (to us) origin for the small, four-wheeled cart used to transport an assortment of grip stuff to the set. Perhaps it has to do with the size and shape of the cart or refers to the propensity of certain grips to store uneaten portions of their breakfast burrito there for snacking before lunch.

TAV. Trans American Video, an early part of the Merv Griffin empire and a pioneer in mixing film shows on video in the 1980s.

Teamster. The guy who wears the jacket with the Budweiser Clydesdales on the back. Catchy logo, guys.

Tow plant. A generator or powerplant that is not mounted behind a tractor but on a trailer that requires towing.

UCC-1. Uniform Commercial Code lien-type number 1. Everybody would like to slap one of these on your picture—SAG, DGA, the bond company, the distributor—so that if you don't pay them as agreed, they can take your property. It may not be as easy to foreclose as these folks like to tell you, but try not to have too many of these attached to your project like remoras on a shark.

Webril wipe. A brand name of lint-free, disposable towelette used to clean film and wipe perspiration in the editing room.

WGAw. Acronym for Writers Guild of America west, an outfit that we've lambasted sufficiently in the main text. In fairness, when the WGAw was formed, its members were underpaid, overworked, and ill-appreciated. Times have changed and the WGA should get with the low-budget program or it will end up floating face down like that celebrated journeyman, Joe Gillis, in some Hollywood pool.

Workprint. A positive print made from the camera negative that is used to edit the film. Workprints are usually "one-light" or made without manipulation of the color balance to match tones within a scene so that the color values may vary considerably.

Yard. A place next to the house where you can relax, read this book, and ponder the vagaries of low-budget filmmaking. Also a hundred dollars, which Rick Schmidt thinks is a lot to pay for some motel rooms.

AFTERWORD

Whew, that was a lot of work. We didn't get paid enough for all this writing. We could have made three or four cheap screenplays out of all these words. Unfortunately, like we said, we're not writers. And if we haven't proved that to you by now, nothing in this Afterword is going to convince you.

Yes, we threw in a lot of stuff. Yes, we went back over the same ground a lot. Working the same plot of land and the scatter-gun approach both work. If you've made movies at any budget, you should already know that. Keep planting until something sprouts or keep shooting until you hit it.

We also used a lot of options, precepts, and key points. Is there a preeminent one? Maybe this: As technical as certain aspects of filmmaking may be, it is from script selection (as movies like *Howard the Duck* constantly remind us) to choice of ad art (witness the campaign for *The Last Action Hero*), it remains a hit-and-miss process. Because things will never go exactly as planned, the search for and use of alternatives or just plain going to plan B could be the most critical of your filmmaking decisions. This book is little more than an introduction. There are lots of other books out there, but no matter how thorough they pretend to be, they are all just books. The process itself, only the process, holds all the problems and the answers and keeps them close to the vest. Learning by doing is never truer than with filmmaking, and this book exists only because Hollywood High (the abstraction, not the one at Sunset and Highland) can be such an expensive school to attend.

We hope that you picked up something useful. If not, maybe the bookstore will still give you your money back. If you think that we put in all our secrets, guess again. We don't want to experience sending our set decorator to Hollywood's least-known repository of colorful props, only to find it cleaned out by readers of this book. Actually, we get a special rate (i.e., free) there because we gave the girlfriend of the guy in charge of the warehouse a one-line part and got her into SAG several movies ago; so even if we told you about it, it might not seem like a such a deal.

They don't put "The End" on movies anymore, so we won't do it here. When did they stop doing that, anyway? In the '70s? And we haven't seen a Fellini flick since *Satyricon,* so we don't know if Italian movies still say "Fine." What the hell, on that note, we'll leave you.